AI
Driverless Cars
Chrysalis

Practical Advances in
Artificial Intelligence and Machine Learning

Dr. Lance B. Eliot, MBA, PhD

DEDICATION

To my incredible son, Michael, and my incredible daughter, Lauren.

Forest fortuna adiuvat (from the Latin; good fortune favors the brave).

CONTENTS

Lance B. Eliot

ACKNOWLEDGMENTS

I have been the beneficiary of advice and counsel by many friends, colleagues, family, investors, and many others. I want to thank everyone that has aided me throughout my career. I write from the heart and the head, having experienced first-hand what it means to have others around you that support you during the good times and the tough times.

To Warren Bennis, one of my doctoral advisors and ultimately a colleague, I offer my deepest thanks and appreciation, especially for his calm and insightful wisdom and support.

To Mark Stevens and his generous efforts toward funding and supporting the USC Stevens Center for Innovation.

To Lloyd Greif and the USC Lloyd Greif Center for Entrepreneurial Studies for their ongoing encouragement of founders and entrepreneurs.

To Peter Drucker, William Wang, Aaron Levie, Peter Kim, Jon Kraft, Cindy Crawford, Jenny Ming, Steve Milligan, Chis Underwood, Frank Gehry, Buzz Aldrin, Steve Forbes, Bill Thompson, Dave Dillon, Alan Fuerstman, Larry Ellison, Jim Sinegal, John Sperling, Mark Stevenson, Anand Nallathambi, Thomas Barrack, Jr., and many other innovators and leaders that I have met and gained mightily from doing so.

Thanks to Ed Trainor, Kevin Anderson, James Hickey, Wendell Jones, Ken Harris, DuWayne Peterson, Mike Brown, Jim Thornton, Abhi Beniwal, Al Biland, John Nomura, Eliot Weinman, John Desmond, and many others for their unwavering support during my career.

And most of all thanks as always to Michael and Lauren, for their ongoing support and for having seen me writing and heard much of this material during the many months involved in writing it. To their patience and willingness to listen.

Lance B. Eliot

INTRODUCTION

This is a book that provides the newest innovations and the latest Artificial Intelligence (AI) advances about the emerging nature of AI-based autonomous self-driving driverless cars. Via recent advances in Artificial Intelligence (AI) and Machine Learning (ML), we are nearing the day when vehicles can control themselves and will not require and nor rely upon human intervention to perform their driving tasks (or, that <u>allow</u> for human intervention, but only *require* human intervention in very limited ways).

Similar to my other related books, which I describe in a moment and list the chapters in the Appendix A of this book, I am particularly focused on those advances that pertain to self-driving cars. The phrase "autonomous vehicles" is often used to refer to any kind of vehicle, whether it is ground-based or in the air or sea, and whether it is a cargo hauling trailer truck or a conventional passenger car. Though the aspects described in this book are certainly applicable to all kinds of autonomous vehicles, I am focused more so here on cars.

Indeed, I am especially known for my role in aiding the advancement of self-driving cars, serving currently as the Executive Director of the Cybernetic AI Self-Driving Cars Institute.. In addition to writing software, designing and developing systems and software for self-driving cars, I also speak and write quite a bit about the topic. This book is a collection of some of my more advanced essays. For those of you that might have seen my essays posted elsewhere, I have updated them and integrated them into this book as one handy cohesive package.

You might be interested in companion books that I have written that provide additional key innovations and fundamentals about self-driving cars. Those books are entitled **"Introduction to Driverless Self-Driving Cars,"** **"Advances in AI and Autonomous Vehicles: Cybernetic Self-Driving Cars,"** **"Self-Driving Cars: "The Mother of All AI Projects,"** **"Innovation and Thought Leadership on Self-Driving Driverless Cars,"** **"New Advances in AI Autonomous Driverless Self-Driving Cars,"** **"Autonomous Vehicle Driverless Self-Driving Cars and Artificial Intelligence,"** **"Transformative Artificial Intelligence**

Driverless Self-Driving Cars," "Disruptive Artificial Intelligence and Driverless Self-Driving Cars, and "State-of-the-Art AI Driverless Self-Driving Cars," and "Top Trends in AI Self-Driving Cars," and "AI Innovations and Self-Driving Cars," "Crucial Advances for AI Driverless Cars," "Sociotechnical Insights and AI Driverless Cars," "Pioneering Advances for AI Driverless Cars" and "Leading Edge Trends for AI Driverless Cars," "The Cutting Edge of AI Autonomous Cars" and "The Next Wave of AI Self-Driving Cars" and "Revolutionary Innovations of AI Self-Driving Cars," and "AI Self-Driving Cars Breakthroughs," "Trailblazing Trends for AI Self-Driving Cars," "Ingenious Strides for AI Driverless Cars," "AI Self-Driving Cars Inventiveness," "Visionary Secrets of AI Driverless Cars," "Spearheading AI Self-Driving Cars," "Spurring AI Self-Driving Cars," "Avant-Garde AI Driverless Cars," "AI Self-Driving Cars Evolvement," and "AI Driverless Cars Chrysalis" (they are all available via Amazon). Appendix A has a listing of the chapters covered.

For the introduction herein to this book, I am going to borrow my introduction from those companion books, since it does a good job of laying out the landscape of self-driving cars and my overall viewpoints on the topic. The remainder of the book is all new material that does not appear in the companion books.

INTRODUCTION TO SELF-DRIVING CARS

This is a book about self-driving cars. Someday in the future, we'll all have self-driving cars and this book will perhaps seem antiquated, but right now, we are at the forefront of the self-driving car wave. Daily news bombards us with flashes of new announcements by one car maker or another and leaves the impression that within the next few weeks or maybe months that the self-driving car will be here. A casual non-technical reader would assume from these news flashes that in fact we must be on the cusp of a true self-driving car.

Here's a real news flash: We are still quite a distance from having a true self-driving car. It is years to go before we get there.

Why is that? Because a true self-driving car is akin to a moonshot. In the same manner that getting us to the moon was an incredible feat, likewise is achieving a true self-driving car. Anybody that suggests or even brashly states that the true self-driving car is nearly here should be viewed with great skepticism. Indeed, you'll see that I often tend to use the word "hogwash" or "crock" when I assess much of the decidedly *fake news* about self-driving cars. Those of us on the inside know that what is often reported to the outside is malarkey. Few of the insiders are willing to say so. I have no such hesitation.

Indeed, I've been writing a popular blog post about self-driving cars and hitting hard on those that try to wave their hands and pretend that we are on the imminent verge of true self-driving cars. For many years, I've been known as the AI Insider. Besides writing about AI, I also develop AI software. I do what I describe. It also gives me insights into what others that are doing AI are really doing versus what it is said they are doing.

Many faithful readers had asked me to pull together my insightful short essays and put them into another book, which you are now holding.

For those of you that have been reading my essays over the years, this collection not only puts them together into one handy package, I also updated the essays and added new material. For those of you that are new to the topic of self-driving cars and AI, I hope you find these essays approachable and informative. I also tend to have a writing style with a bit of a voice, and so you'll see that I am times have a wry sense of humor and poke at conformity.

As a former professor and founder of an AI research lab, I for many years wrote in the formal language of academic writing. I published in referred journals and served as an editor for several AI journals. This writing here is not of the nature, and I have adopted a different and more informal style for these essays. That being said, I also do mention from time-to-time more rigorous material on AI and encourage you all to dig into those deeper and more formal materials if so interested.

I am also an AI practitioner. This means that I write AI software for a living. Currently, I head-up the Cybernetics Self-Driving Car Institute, where we are developing AI software for self-driving cars. I am excited to also report that my son, also a software engineer, heads-up our Cybernetics Self-Driving Car Lab. What I have helped to start, and for which he is an integral part, ultimately he will carry long into the future after I have retired. My daughter, a marketing whiz, also is integral to our efforts as head of our Marketing group. She too will carry forward the legacy now being formulated.

For those of you that are reading this book and have a penchant for writing code, you might consider taking a look at the open source code available for self-driving cars. This is a handy place to start learning how to develop AI for self-driving cars. There are also many new educational courses spring forth. There is a growing body of those wanting to learn about and develop self-driving cars, and a growing body of colleges, labs, and other avenues by which you can learn about self-driving cars.

This book will provide a foundation of aspects that I think will get you ready for those kinds of more advanced training opportunities. If you've already taken those classes, you'll likely find these essays especially interesting as they offer a perspective that I am betting few other instructors or faculty offered to you. These are challenging essays that ask you to think beyond the conventional about self-driving cars.

THE MOTHER OF ALL AI PROJECTS

In June 2017, Apple CEO Tim Cook came out and finally admitted that Apple has been working on a self-driving car. As you'll see in my essays, Apple was enmeshed in secrecy about their self-driving car efforts. We have only been able to read the tea leaves and guess at what Apple has been up to. The notion of an iCar has been floating for quite a while, and self-driving engineers and researchers have been signing tight-lipped Non-Disclosure Agreements (NDA's) to work on projects at Apple that were as shrouded in mystery as any military invasion plans might be.

Tim Cook said something that many others in the Artificial Intelligence (AI) field have been saying, namely, the creation of a self-driving car has got to be the mother of all AI projects. In other words, it is in fact a tremendous moonshot for AI. If a self-driving car can be crafted and the AI works as we hope, it means that we have made incredible strides with AI and that therefore it opens many other worlds of potential breakthrough accomplishments that AI can solve.

Is this hyperbole? Am I just trying to make AI seem like a miracle worker and so provide self-aggrandizing statements for those of us writing the AI software for self-driving cars? No, it is not hyperbole. Developing a true self-driving car is really, really, really hard to do. Let me take a moment to explain why. As a side note, I realize that the Apple CEO is known for at times uttering hyperbole, and he had previously said for example that the year 2012 was "the mother of all years," and he had said that the release of iOS 10 was "the mother of all releases" – all of which does suggest he likes to use the handy "mother of" expression. But, I assure you, in terms of true self-driving cars, he has hit the nail on the head. For sure.

When you think about a moonshot and how we got to the moon, there are some identifiable characteristics and those same aspects can be applied to creating a true self-driving car. You'll notice that I keep putting the word "true" in front of the self-driving car expression. I do so because as per my essay about the various levels of self-driving cars, there are some self-driving cars that are only somewhat of a self-driving car. The somewhat versions are ones that require a human driver to be ready to intervene. In my view, that's not a true self-driving car. A true self-driving car is one that requires no human driver intervention at all. It is a car that can entirely undertake via automation the driving task without any human driver needed. This is the essence of what is known as a Level 5 self-driving car. We are currently at the Level 2 and Level 3 mark, and not yet at Level 5.

Getting to the moon involved aspects such as having big stretch goals, incremental progress, experimentation, innovation, and so on. Let's review how this applied to the moonshot of the bygone era, and how it applies to the self-driving car moonshot of today.

Big Stretch Goal

Trying to take a human and deliver the human to the moon, and bring them back, safely, was an extremely large stretch goal at the time. No one knew whether it could be done. The technology wasn't available yet. The cost was huge. The determination would need to be fierce. Etc. To reach a Level 5 self-driving car is going to be the same. It is a big stretch goal. We can readily get to the Level 3, and we are able to see the Level 4 just up ahead, but a Level 5 is still an unknown as to if it is doable. It should eventually be doable and in the same way that we thought we'd eventually get to the moon, but when it will occur is a different story.

Incremental Progress

Getting to the moon did not happen overnight in one fell swoop. It took years and years of incremental progress to get there. Likewise for self-driving cars. Google has famously been striving to get to the Level 5, and pretty much been willing to forgo dealing with the intervening levels, but most of the other self-driving car makers are doing the incremental route. Let's get a good Level 2 and a somewhat Level 3 going. Then, let's improve the Level 3 and get a somewhat Level 4 going. Then, let's improve the Level 4 and finally arrive at a Level 5. This seems to be the prevalent way that we are going to achieve the true self-driving car.

Experimentation

You likely know that there were various experiments involved in perfecting the approach and technology to get to the moon. As per making incremental progress, we first tried to see if we could get a rocket to go into space and safety return, then put a monkey in there, then with a human, then we went all the way to the moon but didn't land, and finally we arrived at the mission that actually landed on the moon. Self-driving cars are the same way. We are doing simulations of self-driving cars. We do testing of self-driving cars on private land under controlled situations. We do testing of self-driving cars on public roadways, often having to meet regulatory requirements including for example having an engineer or equivalent in the car to take over the controls if needed. And so on. Experiments big and small are needed to figure out what works and what doesn't.

Innovation

There are already some advances in AI that are allowing us to progress toward self-driving cars. We are going to need even more advances. Innovation in all aspects of technology are going to be required to achieve a true self-driving car. By no means do we already have everything in-hand that we need to get there. Expect new inventions and new approaches, new algorithms, etc.

Setbacks

Most of the pundits are avoiding talking about potential setbacks in the progress toward self-driving cars. Getting to the moon involved many setbacks, some of which you never have heard of and were buried at the time so as to not dampen enthusiasm and funding for getting to the moon. A recurring theme in many of my included essays is that there are going to be setbacks as we try to arrive at a true self-driving car. Take a deep breath and be ready. I just hope the setbacks don't completely stop progress. I am sure that it will cause progress to alter in a manner that we've not yet seen in the self-driving car field. I liken the self-driving car of today to the excitement everyone had for Uber when it first got going. Today, we have a different view of Uber and with each passing day there are more regulations to the ride sharing business and more concerns raised. The darling child only stays a darling until finally that child acts up. It will happen the same with self-driving cars.

SELF-DRIVING CARS CHALLENGES

But what exactly makes things so hard to have a true self-driving car, you might be asking. You have seen cruise control for years and years. You've lately seen cars that can do parallel parking. You've seen YouTube videos of Tesla drivers that put their hands out the window as their car zooms along the highway, and seen to therefore be in a self-driving car. Aren't we just needing to put a few more sensors onto a car and then we'll have in-hand a true self-driving car? Nope.

Consider for a moment the nature of the driving task. We don't just let anyone at any age drive a car. Worldwide, most countries won't license a driver until the age of 18, though many do allow a learner's permit at the age of 15 or 16. Some suggest that a younger age would be physically too small to reach the controls of the car. Though this might be the case, we could easily adjust the controls to allow for younger aged and thus smaller stature. It's not their physical size that matters. It's their cognitive development that matters.

To drive a car, you need to be able to reason about the car, what the car can and cannot do. You need to know how to operate the car. You need to know about how other cars on the road drive. You need to know what is allowed in driving such as speed limits and driving within marked lanes. You need to be able to react to situations and be able to avoid getting into accidents. You need to ascertain when to hit your brakes, when to steer clear of a pedestrian, and how to keep from ramming that motorcyclist that just cut you off.

Many of us had taken courses on driving. We studied about driving and took driver training. We had to take a test and pass it to be able to drive. The point being that though most adults take the driving task for granted, and we often "mindlessly" drive our cars, there is a significant amount of cognitive effort that goes into driving a car. After a while, it becomes second nature. You don't especially think about how you drive, you just do it. But, if you watch a novice driver, say a teenager learning to drive, you suddenly realize that there is a lot more complexity to it than we seem to realize.

Furthermore, driving is a very serious task. I recall when my daughter and son first learned to drive. They are both very conscientious people. They wanted to make sure that whatever they did, they did well, and that they did not harm anyone. Every day, when you get into a car, it is probably around 4,000 pounds of hefty metal and plastics (about two tons), and it is a lethal weapon. Think about it. You drive down the street in an object that weighs two tons and with the engine it can accelerate and ram into anything you want to hit. The damage a car can inflict is very scary. Both my children were surprised that they were being given the right to maneuver this monster of a beast that could cause tremendous harm entirely by merely letting go of the steering wheel for a moment or taking your eyes off the road.

In fact, in the United States alone there are about 30,000 deaths per year by auto accidents, which is around 100 per day. Given that there are about 263 million cars in the United States, I am actually more amazed that the number of fatalities is not a lot higher. During my morning commute, I look at all the thousands of cars on the freeway around me, and I think that if all of them decided to go zombie and drive in a crazy maniac way, there would be many people dead. Somehow, incredibly, each day, most people drive relatively safely. To me, that's a miracle right there. Getting millions and millions of people to be safe and sane when behind the wheel of a two ton mobile object, it's a feat that we as a society should admire with pride.

So, hopefully you are in agreement that the driving task requires a great deal of cognition. You don't' need to be especially smart to drive a car, and we've done quite a bit to make car driving viable for even the average dolt. There isn't an IQ test that you need to take to drive a car. If you can read and write, and pass a test, you pretty much can legally drive a car. There are of course some that drive a car and are not legally permitted to do so, plus there are private areas such as farms where drivers are young, but for public roadways in the United States, you can be generally of average intelligence (or less) and be able to legally drive.

This though makes it seem like the cognitive effort must not be much. If the cognitive effort was truly hard, wouldn't we only have Einstein's that could drive a car? We have made sure to keep the driving task as simple as we can, by making the controls easy and relatively standardized, and by having roads that are relatively standardized, and so on. It is as though Disneyland has put their Autopia into the real-world, by us all as a society agreeing that roads will be a certain way, and we'll all abide by the various rules of driving.

A modest cognitive task by a human is still something that stymies AI. You certainly know that AI has been able to beat chess players and be good at other kinds of games. This type of narrow cognition is not what car driving is about. Car driving is much wider. It requires knowledge about the world, which a chess playing AI system does not need to know. The cognitive aspects of driving are on the one hand seemingly simple, but at the same time require layer upon layer of knowledge about cars, people, roads, rules, and a myriad of other "common sense" aspects. We don't have any AI systems today that have that same kind of breadth and depth of awareness and knowledge.

As revealed in my essays, the self-driving car of today is using trickery to do particular tasks. It is all very narrow in operation. Plus, it currently assumes that a human driver is ready to intervene. It is like a child that we have taught to stack blocks, but we are needed to be right there in case the child stacks them too high and they begin to fall over. AI of today is brittle, it is narrow, and it does not approach the cognitive abilities of humans. This is why the true self-driving car is somewhere out in the future.

Another aspect to the driving task is that it is not solely a mind exercise. You do need to use your senses to drive. You use your eyes a vision sensors to see the road ahead. You vision capability is like a streaming video, which your brain needs to continually analyze as you drive. Where is the road? Is there a pedestrian in the way? Is there another car ahead of you? Your senses are relying a flood of info to your brain. Self-driving cars are trying to do the same, by using cameras, radar, ultrasound, and lasers. This is an attempt at mimicking how humans have senses and sensory apparatus.

Thus, the driving task is mental and physical. You use your senses, you use your arms and legs to manipulate the controls of the car, and you use your brain to assess the sensory info and direct your limbs to act upon the controls of the car. This all happens instantly. If you've ever perhaps gotten something in your eye and only had one eye available to drive with, you suddenly realize how dependent upon vision you are. If you have a broken foot with a cast, you suddenly realize how hard it is to control the brake pedal and the accelerator. If you've taken medication and your brain is maybe sluggish, you suddenly realize how much mental strain is required to drive a car.

An AI system that plays chess only needs to be focused on playing chess. The physical aspects aren't important because usually a human moves the chess pieces or the chessboard is shown on an electronic display. Using AI for a more life-and-death task such as analyzing MRI images of patients, this again does not require physical capabilities and instead is done by examining images of bits.

Driving a car is a true life-and-death task. It is a use of AI that can easily and at any moment produce death. For those colleagues of mine that are developing this AI, as am I, we need to keep in mind the somber aspects of this. We are producing software that will have in its virtual hands the lives of the occupants of the car, and the lives of those in other nearby cars, and the lives of nearby pedestrians, etc. Chess is not usually a life-or-death matter.

Driving is all around us. Cars are everywhere. Most of today's AI applications involve only a small number of people. Or, they are behind the scenes and we as humans have other recourse if the AI messes up. AI that is driving a car at 80 miles per hour on a highway had better not mess up. The consequences are grave. Multiply this by the number of cars, if we could put magically self-driving into every car in the USA, we'd have AI running in the 263 million cars. That's a lot of AI spread around. This is AI on a massive scale that we are not doing today and that offers both promise and potential peril.

There are some that want AI for self-driving cars because they envision a world without any car accidents. They envision a world in which there is no car congestion and all cars cooperate with each other. These are wonderful utopian visions.

They are also very misleading. The adoption of self-driving cars is going to be incremental and not overnight. We cannot economically just junk all existing cars. Nor are we going to be able to affordably retrofit existing cars. It is more likely that self-driving cars will be built into new cars and that over many years of gradual replacement of existing cars that we'll see the mix of self-driving cars become substantial in the real-world.

In these essays, I have tried to offer technological insights without being overly technical in my description, and also blended the business, societal, and economic aspects too. Technologists need to consider the non-technological impacts of what they do. Non-technologists should be aware of what is being developed.

We all need to work together to collectively be prepared for the enormous disruption and transformative aspects of true self-driving cars. We all need to be involved in this mother of all AI projects.

WHAT THIS BOOK PROVIDES

What does this book provide to you? It introduces many of the key elements about self-driving cars and does so with an AI based perspective. I weave together technical and non-technical aspects, readily going from being concerned about the cognitive capabilities of the driving task and how the technology is embodying this into self-driving cars, and in the next breath I discuss the societal and economic aspects.

They are all intertwined because that's the way reality is. You cannot separate out the technology per se, and instead must consider it within the milieu of what is being invented and innovated, and do so with a mindset towards the contemporary mores and culture that shape what we are doing and what we hope to do.

WHY THIS BOOK

I wrote this book to try and bring to the public view many aspects about self-driving cars that nobody seems to be discussing.

For business leaders that are either involved in making self-driving cars or that are going to leverage self-driving cars, I hope that this book will enlighten you as to the risks involved and ways in which you should be strategizing about how to deal with those risks.

For entrepreneurs, startups and other businesses that want to enter into the self-driving car market that is emerging, I hope this book sparks your interest in doing so, and provides some sense of what might be prudent to pursue.

For researchers that study self-driving cars, I hope this book spurs your interest in the risks and safety issues of self-driving cars, and also nudges you toward conducting research on those aspects.

For students in computer science or related disciplines, I hope this book will provide you with interesting and new ideas and material, for which you might conduct research or provide some career direction insights for you.

For AI companies and high-tech companies pursuing self-driving cars, this book will hopefully broaden your view beyond just the mere coding and development needed to make self-driving cars.

For all readers, I hope that you will find the material in this book to be stimulating. Some of it will be repetitive of things you already know. But I am pretty sure that you'll also find various eureka moments whereby you'll discover a new technique or approach that you had not earlier thought of. I am also betting that there will be material that forces you to rethink some of your current practices.

I am not saying you will suddenly have an epiphany and change what you are doing. I do think though that you will reconsider or perhaps revisit what you are doing.

For anyone choosing to use this book for teaching purposes, please take a look at my suggestions for doing so, as described in the Appendix. I have found the material handy in courses that I have taught, and likewise other faculty have told me that they have found the material handy, in some cases as extended readings and in other instances as a core part of their course (depending on the nature of the class).

In my writing for this book, I have tried carefully to blend both the practitioner and the academic styles of writing. It is not as dense as is typical academic journal writing, but at the same time offers depth by going into the nuances and trade-offs of various practices.

The word "deep" is in vogue today, meaning getting deeply into a subject or topic, and so is the word "unpack" which means to tease out the underlying aspects of a subject or topic. I have sought to offer material that addresses an issue or topic by going relatively deeply into it and make sure that it is well unpacked.

Finally, in any book about AI, it is difficult to use our everyday words without having some of them be misinterpreted. Specifically, it is easy to anthropomorphize AI. When I say that an AI system "knows" something, I do not want you to construe that the AI system has sentience and "knows" in the same way that humans do. They aren't that way, as yet. I have tried to use quotes around such words from time-to-time to emphasize that the words I am using should not be misinterpreted to ascribe true human intelligence to the AI systems that we know of today. If I used quotes around all such words, the book would be very difficult to read, and so I am doing so judiciously. Please keep that in mind as you read the material, thanks.

COMPANION BOOKS

If you find this material of interest, you might enjoy these too:

1. **"Introduction to Driverless Self-Driving Cars"** by Dr. Lance Eliot
2. **"Innovation and Thought Leadership on Self-Driving Driverless Cars"** by Dr. Lance Eliot
3. **"Advances in AI and Autonomous Vehicles: Cybernetic Self-Driving Cars"** by Dr. Lance Eliot
4. **"Self-Driving Cars: The Mother of All AI Projects"** by Dr. Lance Eliot
5. **"New Advances in AI Autonomous Driverless Self-Driving Cars"** by Dr. Lance Eliot
6. **"Autonomous Vehicle Driverless Self-Driving Cars and Artificial Intelligence"** by Dr. Lance Eliot and Michael B. Eliot
7. **"Transformative Artificial Intelligence Driverless Self-Driving Cars"** by Dr. Lance Eliot
8. **"Disruptive Artificial Intelligence and Driverless Self-Driving Cars"** by Dr. Lance Eliot
9. "State-of-the-Art AI Driverless Self-Driving Cars" by Dr. Lance Eliot
10. **"Top Trends in AI Self-Driving Cars"** by Dr. Lance Eliot
11. **"AI Innovations and Self-Driving Cars"** by Dr. Lance Eliot
12. **"Crucial Advances for AI Driverless Cars"** by Dr. Lance Eliot
13. **"Sociotechnical Insights and AI Driverless Cars"** by Dr. Lance Eliot.
14. **"Pioneering Advances for AI Driverless Cars"** by Dr. Lance Eliot
15. **"Leading Edge Trends for AI Driverless Cars"** by Dr. Lance Eliot
16. **"The Cutting Edge of AI Autonomous Cars"** by Dr. Lance Eliot
17. **"The Next Wave of AI Self-Driving Cars"** by Dr. Lance Eliot
18. **"Revolutionary Innovations of AI Driverless Cars"** by Dr. Lance Eliot
19. **"AI Self-Driving Cars Breakthroughs"** by Dr. Lance Eliot
20. **"Trailblazing Trends for AI Self-Driving Cars"** by Dr. Lance Eliot
21. **"Ingenious Strides for AI Driverless Cars"** by Dr. Lance Eliot
22. **"AI Self-Driving Cars Inventiveness"** by Dr. Lance Eliot
23. **"Visionary Secrets of AI Driverless Cars"** by Dr. Lance Eliot
24. **"Spearheading AI Self-Driving Cars"** by Dr. Lance Eliot
25. **"Spurring AI Self-Driving Cars"** by Dr. Lance Eliot
26. **"Avant-Garde AI Driverless Cars"** by Dr. Lance Eliot
27. **"AI Self-Driving Cars Evolvement"** by Dr. Lance Eliot
28. **"AI Driverless Cars Chrysalis"** by Dr. Lance Eliot

These books are available on Amazon and at other major global booksellers.

CHAPTER 1

ELIOT FRAMEWORK FOR AI SELF-DRIVING CARS

CHAPTER 1

ELIOT FRAMEWORK FOR
AI SELF-DRIVING CARS

This chapter is a core foundational aspect for understanding AI self-driving cars and I have used this same chapter in several of my other books to introduce the reader to essential elements of this field. Once you've read this chapter, you'll be prepared to read the rest of the material since the foundational essence of the components of autonomous AI driverless self-driving cars will have been established for you.

———

When I give presentations about self-driving cars and teach classes on the topic, I have found it helpful to provide a framework around which the various key elements of self-driving cars can be understood and organized (see diagram at the end of this chapter). The framework needs to be simple enough to convey the overarching elements, but at the same time not so simple that it belies the true complexity of self-driving cars. As such, I am going to describe the framework here and try to offer in a thousand words (or more!) what the framework diagram itself intends to portray.

The core elements on the diagram are numbered for ease of reference. The numbering does not suggest any kind of prioritization of the elements. Each element is crucial. Each element has a purpose, and otherwise would not be included in the framework. For some self-driving cars, a particular element might be more important or somehow distinguished in comparison to other self-driving cars.

You could even use the framework to rate a particular self-driving car, doing so by gauging how well it performs in each of the elements of the framework. I will describe each of the elements, one at a time. After doing so, I'll discuss aspects that illustrate how the elements interact and perform during the overall effort of a self-driving car.

At the Cybernetic Self-Driving Car Institute, we use the framework to keep track of what we are working on, and how we are developing software that fills in what is needed to achieve Level 5 self-driving cars.

D-01: Sensor Capture

Let's start with the one element that often gets the most attention in the press about self-driving cars, namely, the sensory devices for a self-driving car.

On the framework, the box labeled as D-01 indicates "Sensor Capture" and refers to the processes of the self-driving car that involve collecting data from the myriad of sensors that are used for a self-driving car. The types of devices typically involved are listed, such as the use of mono cameras, stereo cameras, LIDAR devices, radar systems, ultrasonic devices, GPS, IMU, and so on.

These devices are tasked with obtaining data about the status of the self-driving car and the world around it. Some of the devices are continually providing updates, while others of the devices await an indication by the self-driving car that the device is supposed to collect data. The data might be first transformed in some fashion by the device itself, or it might instead be fed directly into the sensor capture as raw data. At that point, it might be up to the sensor capture processes to do transformations on the data. This all varies depending upon the nature of the devices being used and how the devices were designed and developed.

D-02: Sensor Fusion

Imagine that your eyeballs receive visual images, your nose receives odors, your ears receive sounds, and in essence each of your distinct sensory devices is getting some form of input. The input befits the nature of the device. Likewise, for a self-driving car, the cameras provide visual images, the radar returns radar reflections, and so on.

Each device provides the data as befits what the device does.

At some point, using the analogy to humans, you need to merge together what your eyes see, what your nose smells, what your ears hear, and piece it all together into a larger sense of what the world is all about and what is happening around you. Sensor fusion is the action of taking the singular aspects from each of the devices and putting them together into a larger puzzle.

Sensor fusion is a tough task. There are some devices that might not be working at the time of the sensor capture. Or, there might some devices that are unable to report well what they have detected. Again, using a human analogy, suppose you are in a dark room and so your eyes cannot see much. At that point, you might need to rely more so on your ears and what you hear. The same is true for a self-driving car. If the cameras are obscured due to snow and sleet, it might be that the radar can provide a greater indication of what the external conditions consist of.

In the case of a self-driving car, there can be a plethora of such sensory devices. Each is reporting what it can. Each might have its difficulties. Each might have its limitations, such as how far ahead it can detect an object. All of these limitations need to be considered during the sensor fusion task.

D-03: Virtual World Model

For humans, we presumably keep in our minds a model of the world around us when we are driving a car. In your mind, you know that the car is going at say 60 miles per hour and that you are on a freeway. You have a model in your mind that your car is surrounded by other cars, and that there are lanes to the freeway. Your model is not only based on what you can see, hear, etc., but also what you know about the nature of the world. You know that at any moment that car ahead of you can smash on its brakes, or the car behind you can ram into your car, or that the truck in the next lane might swerve into your lane.

The AI of the self-driving car needs to have a virtual world model, which it then keeps updated with whatever it is receiving from the sensor fusion, which received its input from the sensor capture and the sensory devices.

D-04: System Action Plan

By having a virtual world model, the AI of the self-driving car is able to keep track of where the car is and what is happening around the car. In addition, the AI needs to determine what to do next. Should the self-driving car hit its brakes? Should the self-driving car stay in its lane or swerve into the lane to the left? Should the self-driving car accelerate or slow down?

A system action plan needs to be prepared by the AI of the self-driving car. The action plan specifies what actions should be taken. The actions need to pertain to the status of the virtual world model. Plus, the actions need to be realizable.

This realizability means that the AI cannot just assert that the self-driving car should suddenly sprout wings and fly. Instead, the AI must be bound by whatever the self-driving car can actually do, such as coming to a halt in a distance of X feet at a speed of Y miles per hour, rather than perhaps asserting that the self-driving car come to a halt in 0 feet as though it could instantaneously come to a stop while it is in motion.

D-05: Controls Activation

The system action plan is implemented by activating the controls of the car to act according to what the plan stipulates. This might mean that the accelerator control is commanded to increase the speed of the car. Or, the steering control is commanded to turn the steering wheel 30 degrees to the left or right.

One question arises as to whether or not the controls respond as they are commanded to do. In other words, suppose the AI has commanded the accelerator to increase, but for some reason it does not do so. Or, maybe it tries to do so, but the speed of the car does not increase. The controls activation feeds back into the virtual world model, and simultaneously the virtual world model is getting updated from the sensors, the sensor capture, and the sensor fusion. This allows the AI to ascertain what has taken place as a result of the controls being commanded to take some kind of action.

By the way, please keep in mind that though the diagram seems to have a linear progression to it, the reality is that these are all aspects of the self-driving car that are happening in parallel and simultaneously. The sensors are capturing data, meanwhile the sensor fusion is taking place, meanwhile the virtual model is being updated, meanwhile the system action plan is being formulated and reformulated, meanwhile the controls are being activated.

This is the same as a human being that is driving a car. They are eyeballing the road, meanwhile they are fusing in their mind the sights, sounds, etc., meanwhile their mind is updating their model of the world around them, meanwhile they are formulating an action plan of what to do, and meanwhile they are pushing their foot onto the pedals and steering the car. In the normal course of driving a car, you are doing all of these at once. I mention this so that when you look at the diagram, you will think of the boxes as processes that are all happening at the same time, and not as though only one happens and then the next.

They are shown diagrammatically in a simplistic manner to help comprehend what is taking place. You though should also realize that they are working in parallel and simultaneous with each other. This is a tough aspect in that the inter-element communications involve latency and other aspects that must be taken into account. There can be delays in one element updating and then sharing its latest status with other elements.

D-06: Automobile & CAN

Contemporary cars use various automotive electronics and a Controller Area Network (CAN) to serve as the components that underlie the driving aspects of a car. There are Electronic Control Units (ECU's) which control subsystems of the car, such as the engine, the brakes, the doors, the windows, and so on.

The elements D-01, D-02, D-03, D-04, D-05 are layered on top of the D-06, and must be aware of the nature of what the D-06 is able to do and not do.

D-07: In-Car Commands

Humans are going to be occupants in self-driving cars. In a Level 5 self-driving car, there must be some form of communication that takes place between the humans and the self-driving car. For example, I go into a self-driving car and tell it that I want to be driven over to Disneyland, and along the way I want to stop at In-and-Out Burger. The self-driving car now parses what I've said and tries to then establish a means to carry out my wishes.

In-car commands can happen at any time during a driving journey. Though my example was about an in-car command when I first got into my self-driving car, it could be that while the self-driving car is carrying out the journey that I change my mind. Perhaps after getting stuck in traffic, I tell the self-driving car to forget about getting the burgers and just head straight over to the theme park. The self-driving car needs to be alert to in-car commands throughout the journey.

D-08: V2X Communications

We will ultimately have self-driving cars communicating with each other, doing so via V2V (Vehicle-to-Vehicle) communications. We will also have self-driving cars that communicate with the roadways and other aspects of the transportation infrastructure, doing so via V2I (Vehicle-to-Infrastructure).

The variety of ways in which a self-driving car will be communicating with other cars and infrastructure is being called V2X, whereby the letter X means whatever else we identify as something that a car should or would want to communicate with. The V2X communications will be taking place simultaneous with everything else on the diagram, and those other elements will need to incorporate whatever it gleans from those V2X communications.

D-09: Deep Learning

The use of Deep Learning permeates all other aspects of the self-driving car. The AI of the self-driving car will be using deep learning to do a better job at the systems action plan, and at the controls activation, and at the sensor fusion, and so on.

Currently, the use of artificial neural networks is the most prevalent form of deep learning. Based on large swaths of data, the neural networks attempt to "learn" from the data and therefore direct the efforts of the self-driving car accordingly.

D-10: Tactical AI

Tactical AI is the element of dealing with the moment-to-moment driving of the self-driving car. Is the self-driving car staying in its lane of the freeway? Is the car responding appropriately to the controls commands? Are the sensory devices working?

For human drivers, the tactical equivalent can be seen when you watch a novice driver such as a teenager that is first driving. They are focused on the mechanics of the driving task, keeping their eye on the road while also trying to properly control the car.

D-11: Strategic AI

The Strategic AI aspects of a self-driving car are dealing with the larger picture of what the self-driving car is trying to do. If I had asked that the self-driving car take me to Disneyland, there is an overall journey map that needs to be kept and maintained.

There is an interaction between the Strategic AI and the Tactical AI. The Strategic AI is wanting to keep on the mission of the driving, while the Tactical AI is focused on the particulars underway in the driving effort. If the Tactical AI seems to wander away from the overarching mission, the Strategic AI wants to see why and get things back on track. If the Tactical AI realizes that there is something amiss on the self-driving car, it needs to alert the Strategic AI accordingly and have an adjustment to the overarching mission that is underway.

D-12: Self-Aware AI

Very few of the self-driving cars being developed are including a Self-Aware AI element, which we at the Cybernetic Self-Driving Car Institute believe is crucial to Level 5 self-driving cars.

The Self-Aware AI element is intended to watch over itself, in the sense that the AI is making sure that the AI is working as intended. Suppose you had a human driving a car, and they were starting to drive erratically. Hopefully, their own self-awareness would make them realize they themselves are driving poorly, such as perhaps starting to fall asleep after having been driving for hours on end. If you had a passenger in the car, they might be able to alert the driver if the driver is starting to do something amiss. This is exactly what the Self-Aware

AI element tries to do, it becomes the overseer of the AI, and tries to detect when the AI has become faulty or confused, and then find ways to overcome the issue.

D-13: Economic

The economic aspects of a self-driving car are not per se a technology aspect of a self-driving car, but the economics do indeed impact the nature of a self-driving car. For example, the cost of outfitting a self-driving car with every kind of possible sensory device is prohibitive, and so choices need to be made about which devices are used. And, for those sensory devices chosen, whether they would have a full set of features or a more limited set of features.

We are going to have self-driving cars that are at the low-end of a consumer cost point, and others at the high-end of a consumer cost point. You cannot expect that the self-driving car at the low-end is going to be as robust as the one at the high-end. I realize that many of the self-driving car pundits are acting as though all self-driving cars will be the same, but they won't be. Just like anything else, we are going to have self-driving cars that have a range of capabilities. Some will be better than others. Some will be safer than others. This is the way of the real-world, and so we need to be thinking about the economics aspects when considering the nature of self-driving cars.

D-14: Societal

This component encompasses the societal aspects of AI which also impacts the technology of self-driving cars. For example, the famous Trolley Problem involves what choices should a self-driving car make when faced with life-and-death matters. If the self-driving car is about to either hit a child standing in the roadway, or instead ram into a tree at the side of the road and possibly kill the humans in the self-driving car, which choice should be made?

We need to keep in mind the societal aspects will underlie the AI of the self-driving car. Whether we are aware of it explicitly or not, the AI will have embedded into it various societal assumptions.

D-15: Innovation

I included the notion of innovation into the framework because we can anticipate that whatever a self-driving car consists of, it will continue to be innovated over time. The self-driving cars coming out in the next several years will undoubtedly be different and less innovative than the versions that come out in ten years hence, and so on.

Framework Overall

For those of you that want to learn about self-driving cars, you can potentially pick a particular element and become specialized in that aspect. Some engineers are focusing on the sensory devices. Some engineers focus on the controls activation. And so on. There are specialties in each of the elements.

Researchers are likewise specializing in various aspects. For example, there are researchers that are using Deep Learning to see how best it can be used for sensor fusion. There are other researchers that are using Deep Learning to derive good System Action Plans. Some are studying how to develop AI for the Strategic aspects of the driving task, while others are focused on the Tactical aspects.

A well-prepared all-around software developer that is involved in self-driving cars should be familiar with all of the elements, at least to the degree that they know what each element does. This is important since whatever piece of the pie that the software developer works on, they need to be knowledgeable about what the other elements are doing.

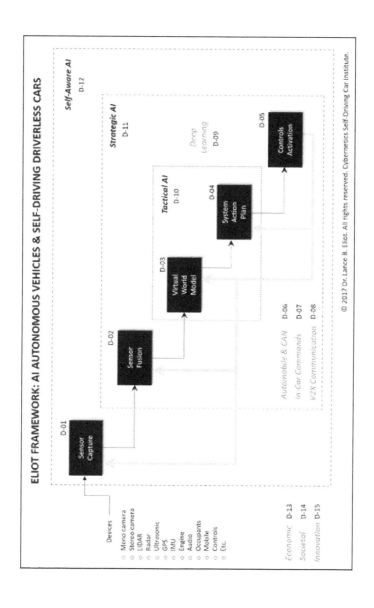

ELIOT FRAMEWORK: AI AUTONOMOUS VEHICLES & SELF-DRIVING DRIVERLESS CARS

Self-Aware AI
D-12

Strategic AI
D-11

Deep Learning
D-09

Tactical AI
D-1D

Controls Activation
D-05

System Action Plan
D-04

Virtual World Model
D-03

Sensor Fusion
D-02

Sensor Capture
D-01

Automobile & CAN   D-06
In-Car Commands   D-07
V2X Communication   D-08

Devices
○ Mono camera
○ Stereo camera
○ LIDAR
○ Radar
○ Ultrasonic
○ GPS
○ IMU
○ Engine
○ Audio
○ Occupants
○ Mobile
○ Controls
○ Etc.

Economic   D-13
Societal   D-14
Innovation   D-15

CHAPTER 2

OBJECT POSES
AND
AI SELF-DRIVING CARS

CHAPTER 2

OBJECT POSES
AND AI SELF-DRIVING CARS

Take an object nearby you and turn it upside down.

Please don't do this to something or someone that would get upset at your suddenly turning them upside down. Assuming that you've turned an object upside down, look at it. Do you still know what the object is? I'd bet that you do.

But why would you? If you were used to seeing it right-side up, presumably you should be baffled at what the object is, now that you've turned it upside down. It doesn't look like it did a moment ago. A moment ago, the bottom was, well, on the bottom. The top was on the top. Now, the bottom is on the top, and the top is on the bottom. I dare say that you should be completely puzzled about the object. It is unrecognizable now that it has been flipped over.

I'm guessing that you are puzzled that I would even suggest that you should be puzzled. Of course, you recognize what the object is. No big deal. It seems silly perhaps to assert that the mere act of turning the object upside down should impact your ability to recognize the object. You might insist that the object is still the same object that it was a moment ago. No change has occurred. It is simply reoriented.

Not so fast. Your ability as a grown adult is helping you quite a bit on this seemingly innocuous task. For you, it has been years upon years of cognitive maturation that makes things so easy to perceive an object when reoriented.

I could get you to falter somewhat by showing you an object that I had hidden behind my back and suddenly showed it to you, only showing it to you while it is being held upside down. Without first my showing it to you in a right-side up posture, the odds are that it would take you a few moments to figure out what the upside-down object was.

A Father's Story About Reorienting Objects

This discussion causes me to hark back to when my daughter was quite young.

She had a favorite doll that had a big grin on the doll, permanently in place. There were a series of small buttons that shaped the mouth and it was curved in a manner that made it look like a smiley face type of grin. When you looked at the doll, you almost instinctively would react to the wide smile and it would spark you to smile too. She really liked the doll, it was her favorite toy and not to be trifled with.

One day, we were sitting at the dinner table and I opted to turn the doll upside down. I asked my daughter whether the doll was smiling or whether the doll was frowning. Though I realize you cannot at this moment see the doll that I am referring to, I'm sure you realize that the doll was still smiling, but when the doll was turned upside down, the smile would be upside down and resemble a frown.

My daughter said that the doll was sad, it was frowning.

I turned the doll right-side up.

And now what is the expression, I asked my daughter.

The doll is smiling again, she said.

I explained that the doll had always been smiling, even when turned upside down. This got a look of puzzlement on my daughter's face. By the way, I was potentially on the verge of trifling with her favored toy, so I assure you that I carried out this activity with great respect and care.

She challenged me to turn the doll upside down again. I did so.

My daughter stood-up, and tried to do a handstand, flipping herself upside down. Upon quasi-doing so, she gazed at the doll, and could see that the doll was still smiling. She agreed that the doll was still smiling and retracted her earlier indication that it had been frowning.

I waited about a week and tried to pull this stunt again. This time, she responded instantly that the doll was still smiling, even after I had turned it upside down. She obviously had caught on.

When I tried this once again about two weeks later, she said the doll was sad. This surprised me and I wondered if she had perchance forgotten our earlier stints. When I asked her why the doll was sad, she told me it was because I keep turning her upside down and she's not fond of my doing so. Ha! I was put into my place.

The overall point herein is that when we are very young, being able to discern objects that are upside down can be quite difficult. You've not yet modeled in your mind the notion of reorienting objects and being able to rotate them, doing so to then recognize them as readily. Sure, my daughter knew that the doll was still the doll, but the smile that was a frown suggested an as-yet developed sense of reorienting of objects.

Human Mental Capabilities in Reorienting Objects

What makes our learning capabilities so impressive is that you don't just fixate on a particular object and instead you ultimately generalize to objects all told. My daughter was able to not only figure out the doll once it was upside down, she generalized this modeling to be able to then figure out other objects that were turned upside down. If I showed her an object in the right-side up position first, it was usually relatively easy for her to comprehend the object once I had turned it upside down.

Turning an object upside down, prior to presenting it, can be a bit of a challenge to your identifying an object, when presented to someone, even for adults. We are momentarily caught off-guard by the untoward orientation (assuming that you don't normally see it upside down).

Your mind tries to examine the upside-down object and perhaps reorients the object in your mind, creating a picture in your mind, and flipping the picture to a right-side up orientation to make sense of it. You then match the reoriented mental image of the object to your stored right-side up images, and voila, you identify what the real-world object is.

Or, it could be that the mind takes a known right-side up image that's already in its stored memory, and for which you believe it might be, and flips over the stored image that's in your head, and then matches it to the object that you are seeing positioned as upside down, trying to decide if it is indeed that object. That's another plausible way to do this.

There have been lots of cognitive and psychological experiments trying to figure out the mental mechanisms in the brain that aid us when dealing with the reorientation of objects. Theories abound about how are brain actually figures these things out. I've so far suggested or implied that we keep an image of objects in our mind. Like a picture. But, that's hard to prove.

Maybe it is some kind of calculus in our minds and there isn't an object image per se being used. It could be a bunch of formulas. Maybe our minds are a vast collection of geometric formulas. Or, it could be a bunch of numbers. Perhaps our minds turn everything into a kind of binary code and there aren't any images per se in our minds (well, I suppose it could be an image represented in a binary code).

The actual brain functioning is still a mystery and other than seemingly considerable and at times clever experiments, we cannot say for absolute certainty how the brain does this for us. Efforts in neuroscience continue to push forward, trying to nail down the mechanical biological and chemical plumbing of the brain.

Range of Reorienting Objects and Their Poses

I've focused on the idea of completely turning an object upside down. That's not the only way to confuse our minds about an object.

You can turn an object on its side, which might also make things hard for you to then recognize the object. Usually, we quickly guess at the object when it is only partially reoriented and can seemingly do a pretty good guess at what it is. Turning the object upside down seems to be a more extreme variant, nonetheless even some milder reorientation can still cause us to pause or maybe even misclassify the object.

If I were to take an object and slowly rotate it, the odds are that you would be able to accurately say what the object is, assuming you watched it during the rotations. When I suddenly show you an object that has already been somewhat rotated, you have no initial basis to use as an anchor, and therefore it is more challenging to figure out what the object might be.

Familiarity plays a big part of this too. If I did a series of rotations of the object, and you were staring at it, your mind seems to be able to get used to those orientations. Thus, if later on, I suddenly spring upon you that same object in a rotated posture, you are more apt to quickly know what it is, due to having seen it earlier in the rotated position.

In that sense, I can essentially train your mind about what an object looks like in a variety of orientations, making it much easier for you to later on recognize it, when it is in one of those orientations. Maybe your mind has taken snapshots of each orientation. Or, maybe your mind is able to apply some kind of mental algorithm to the orientations of that objects. Don't know.

People that deal with a multitude of orientations of objects tend to get better and better at the object reorientation task. I used to work for a CEO that had a trick plane. He would take me up in it, usually on our lunch break at work (our office was nearby an airport). He would do barrel rolls and all kinds of tricky flight maneuvers. I learned right away to not eat lunch before we went on these flights (think about the vaunted "vomit comet").

In any case, he was able to "see" the world around us quite well, in spite of the times when we were flying upside down. For me, the world was quite confusing looking when we were upside down. I had a difficult time with it. Then again, I've never been the type to enjoy those roller coaster rides that turn you upside down and try to scare the heck out of you.

AI Self-Driving Cars and Object Orientations in Street Scenes

What does this have to do with AI self-driving cars?

At the Cybernetic AI Self-Driving Car Institute, we are developing AI software for self-driving cars. One of the major concerns that we have, and the auto makers have, and tech firms have, pertains to Machine Learning or Deep Learning that we are all using today, and which tends to be ultra-brittle when it comes to objects that are reoriented.

This is bad because it means that the AI system might either not recognize an object due to the orientation of it, or the AI might misclassify an object, and end-up tragically getting the self-driving car into a precarious situation because of it.

Allow me to elaborate.

I'd like to first clarify and introduce the notion that there are varying levels of AI self-driving cars. The topmost level is considered Level 5. A Level 5 self-driving car is one that is being driven by the AI and there is no human driver involved.

For the design of Level 5 self-driving cars, the auto makers are even removing the gas pedal, brake pedal, and steering wheel, since those are contraptions used by human drivers. The Level 5 self-driving car is not being driven by a human and nor is there an expectation that a human driver will be present in the self-driving car. It's all on the shoulders of the AI to drive the car.

For self-driving cars less than a Level 5, there must be a human driver present in the car. The human driver is currently considered the responsible party for the acts of the car. The AI and the human driver are co-sharing the driving task. In spite of this co-sharing, the human is supposed to remain fully immersed into the driving task and be ready at all times to perform the driving task. I've repeatedly warned about the dangers of this co-sharing arrangement and predicted it will produce many untoward results.

Let's focus herein on the true Level 5 self-driving car. Much of the comments apply to the less than Level 5 self-driving cars too, but the fully autonomous AI self-driving car will receive the most attention in this discussion.

Here's the usual steps involved in the AI driving task:

- Sensor data collection and interpretation
- Sensor fusion
- Virtual world model updating
- AI action planning
- Car controls command issuance

Another key aspect of AI self-driving cars is that they will be driving on our roadways in the midst of human driven cars too. There are some pundits of AI self-driving cars that continually refer to a utopian world in which there are only AI self-driving cars on the public roads. Currently there are about 250+ million conventional cars in the United States alone, and those cars are not going to magically disappear or become true Level 5 AI self-driving cars overnight.

Indeed, the use of human driven cars will last for many years, likely many decades, and the advent of AI self-driving cars will occur while there are still human driven cars on the roads.

This is a crucial point since this means that the AI of self-driving cars needs to be able to contend with not just other AI self-driving cars, but also contend with human driven cars. It is easy to envision a simplistic and rather unrealistic world in which all AI self-driving cars are politely interacting with each other and being civil about roadway interactions. That's not what is going to be happening for the foreseeable future. AI self-driving cars and human driven cars will need to be able to cope with each other.

Returning to the topic of object orientation, let's consider how today's Machine Learning and Deep Learning works, along with why it is considered at times to be ultra-brittle. We'll also mull over how this ultra-brittleness can spell sour outcomes for the emerging AI self-driving cars.

Suppose I decide to craft an Artificial Neural Network (ANN) that will aid in finding street signs, cars, and pedestrians inside of images or video streaming of a camera that is on a self-driving car. Typically, I would start by finding a large dataset of traffic setting images that I could use to train my ANN. We want this ANN to be as full-bodied as we can make it, so we'll have a multitude of layers and compose it of a large number of artificial neurons, thus we might refer to this kind of more robust ANN as a Deep Neural Network (DNN).

Take a look at Figure 1.

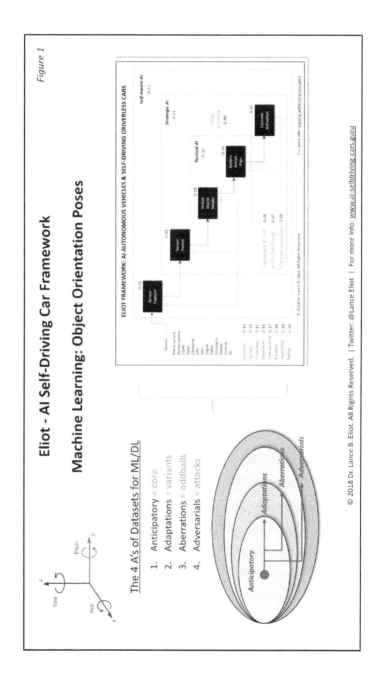

Datasets Essential to Deep Learning

You might wonder how I will come upon the thousands upon thousands of images of traffic scenes. I need a rather large set of images to be able to appropriately train the DNN. I don't want to have to go outside and start taking pictures, since it would take me a long time to do so and be costly to upload them all and store them. My best bet would be to go ahead and use datasets that already exist.

Indeed, some would say that the reason we've seen such great progress in the application of Deep Learning and Machine Learning is because of the efforts by others to create large-scale datasets that we can all use to do our training of the ANN or DNN. We stand on the shoulders of those that went to the trouble to put together those datasets, thanks.

This also though means there is a kind of potential vulnerability that is taking place, one that is not so obvious. If we all use the same datasets, and if those datasets have particular nuances in them, it means that we all are also going to be having a similar impact on our ANN and DNN trainings. I'll in a moment provide you with an example involving military equipment images that can highlight this vulnerability.

Once I've got my dataset or datasets and readied my DNN to be trained, I would run the DNN over and over, trying to get it to find patterns in the images.

I might do so in a supervisory way, wherein I provide an indication of what I want it to find, such as I might give the DNN guidance toward discovering images of school buses or maybe of fire trucks or perhaps scooters. It might be that I opt to do this in an unsupervised fashion and allow the DNN to find whatever it finds, and provide an indication of what those objects that it clusters or classifies are. For example, those yellow lengthy blobs that have big tires and lots of windows are school buses.

I am hoping that the DNN is generalizing sufficiently about the objects, in the sense that if a yellow school bus is bright yellow, it is still a school bus, while if it is maybe a dull yellow due to faded paint and dirt and grime, the DNN should still be classifying it into the school bus category. I mention this because you typically do not have an easy way to make the DNN explain what it is using to find and classify the objects within the image. Instead, you merely hope and assume that if it seems to be able to find those yellow buses, it presumably is using useful criteria to do so.

There is the famous story that highlights the dangers of making this kind of assumption about the manner in which the pattern matching is taking place. The story goes that there were pictures of Russia military equipment, like tanks and cannons, and there were pictures of United States military equipment. Thousands of images that had those kinds of equipment were fed into an ANN. The ANN seemed to be able to discern between the Russian military equipment and the United States military equipment, of which we would presume that it was due to the differences in the shape and designs of their respective tanks and cannons.

Turns out that upon further inspection, the pictures of the Russian military equipment were all grainy and slightly out of focus, while the United States military equipment pictures were crisp and bright. The ANN pattern matched on the background and lighting aspects, rather than the shape of the military equipment itself. This was not readily discerned at first because the same set of images were used to train the ANN and then test it. Thus, the test set were also grainy for the Russian equipment and crisp for the U.S. equipment, misleading one into believing that the ANN was doing a generalized job of gauging the object differences, when it was not doing so.

This highlights an important aspect for those using Machine Learning and Deep Learning, namely trying to ferret out how your ANN or DNN is achieving its pattern matching. If you treat it utterly like a black box, there might be ways in which the pattern matching has landed that won't be satisfactory for use when the ANN or DNN is used in real-world ways.

You might have thought that you did a great job, but once the ANN or DNN is exposed to other images, beyond your datasets, it could be that the characteristics used to classify objects is revealed as brittle and not what you had hoped for.

Considering Deep Learning as Brittle and Ultra-Brittle

By the word "brittle" I am referring to the notion that the ANN or DNN is not doing a full-bodied kind of pattern matching and will therefore falter or fall-down on doing what you presumably want it to do.

In the case of the tanks and cannons, you likely wanted the patterns to be about the shape of the tank, its turret, its muzzle, its treads, etc. Instead, the pattern matching was about the graininess of the images. That's not going to do much good when you try to use the ANN or DNN in a real-world environment to detect whether there is a Russian tank or a United States tank ahead of you.

Let's liken this to my point about the yellow school bus. If the ANN or DNN is pattern matching on the color of yellow, and if perchance all of most of the images in my dataset were of bright yellow school buses, it could be that the matching is being done by that bright yellow color. This means that if I think that my ANN or DNN is good to go, and it encounters a school bus that is old, faded in yellow color, and perhaps covered with grime, the ANN or DNN might declare that the object is not a school bus. A human would tell you it was a school bus, since the human presumably is looking at a variety of characteristics, including the wheels, the shape of the bus, the windows, and the color of the bus.

One of the ways in which the brittleness of the ANN or DNN can be exploited involves making use of adversarial images. The notion is to confuse or mislead the trained ANN or DNN into misclassifying an object.

This might be done by a bad actor, someone hoping to cause the ANN or DNN to falter. They can take an image, make some changes to it, feed it into the ANN or DNN that you've crafted, and potentially get the ANN or DNN to say that the object is something other than what it is.

Perhaps one of the more famous examples of this kind of adversarial trickery involves the turtle image that an ANN or DNN was fooled into believing was actually an image of a gun. This can be done by making changes in the image of the turtle. Those changes are enough to have the ANN or DNN no longer pattern match it to being a frog and instead pattern match it to being a gun. What makes these adversarial attacks so alarming is that the turtle might still look like a turtle to the human eye, and the changes made to fool the ANN or DNN are at the pixel level, being so small that the human eye doesn't readily see the difference.

One of the more startling examples of this adversarial trickery involved a one-pixel change that caused an apparent image of a dog to be classified by a DNN as a cat, which goes to show how potentially brittle these systems can be. Those that study these kinds of attacks will often used "differential evolution" or DE to try and find the least amount of change that is the least apparent to humans, aiming to then fool the ANN or DNN and yet make it very hard for a human eye to realize what has been done.

These changes to images are also often referred to as adversarial perturbations.

Remember that I earlier said that by using the same datasets we are somewhat vulnerable, well, a bad actor can study those datasets too, and try to find ways to undermine or undercut an ANN or DNN that has been trained via the use of those datasets. The dataset giveth and it taketh, one might say. By having large-scale datasets readily available, it means the good actors can more readily develop their ANN or DNN, but it also means that the bad actors can try to figure out ways to subvert those good guy ANN and DNN's, doing so by discovering devious adversarial perturbations.

Not all adversarial perturbations need to be conniving, and we might use the adversarial gambit for good purposes too. When you are testing the outcome of your ANN or DNN training, it would be wise to try and do some adversarial perturbations to see what you can find, meaning that you are trying to use this technique to detect your own brittleness. By doing so, hopefully you will be able to then try to shore-up that brittleness. Might as well use the attack for the purposes of discovery and mitigation.

I've so far offered the notion that the images might differ by the color of the object, such as the variants of yellow for a school bus. A school bus also has a number of wheels and tires, which are somewhat large, relative to smaller vehicles. A scooter only has two wheels and those tires are quite a bit smaller than a buses tire.

Imagine looking at image after image of school buses and trying to figure out what features allow them to formulate in your mind that they are school buses. You want to discover a wide enough set of criteria that it is not going to be brittle, yet you also don't want to be overly broad that you then start classifying say trucks as school buses simply because both of those types of transport have larger tires.

Let's add a twist to this. I told you about my daughter and her doll, involving my flipping the doll upside down and asking my daughter whether she could discern if the doll was smiling or frowning. I was not changing any of the actual features of the doll. It was still the same doll, but it was reoriented. That's the only change I made.

Suppose we trained an ANN or DNN with thousands upon thousands of images of yellow buses. The odds are that the pictures of these yellow buses are primarily all of the same overall orientation, namely driving along on a flat road or maybe in a parked spot, sitting perfectly upright. The bus is right-side up.

You probably would assume that the ANN or DNN is pattern matching in such a manner that it doesn't matter the nature of the orientation of the bus.

You would take it for granted that the ANN or DNN "must" realize that the orientation doesn't matter, a bus is still a bus, regardless at what angle and too when upside down.

If we were to tilt the bus, a human would likely still be able to tell you that it is a school bus. I could probably turn the bus completely upside down, if I could do so, and you'd still be able to discern that it is a school bus. I remember one day I was driving along and drove past an accident scene involving a car that had completely flipped upside down and was sitting at the side of the road. I marveled at seeing a car that was upside down. Notice that I could instantly detect it was a car, there was no confusion in my mind that it was anything other than a car, in spite of the fact that it was entirely upside down.

Fascinating Study of Poses Problems in Machine Learning

A fascinating new study by researchers at Auburn University and Adobe provides a handy warning that orientation should not be taken for granted when training your Deep Learning or Machine Learning system. Researchers Michael Alcorn, Qi Li, Zhitao Gong, Chengfei Wang, Long Mai, Wei-Shinn Ku, and Anh Nguyen investigated the vulnerability of DNN's, doing so by using adversarial techniques, primarily involving rotating or reorienting objects in images. These mainly were DNN's that had been trained on rather popular datasets, such as ImageNet and MS COCO.

One aspect about the rotation or reorienting of an object that you might have noticed herein is that I've been suggesting that the objects are 2D and you are merely tilting them or putting them upside down. Given that for most real-world objects like school buses and cars, they are 3D objects, you can do the rotations or reorienting in three dimensions, altering the yaw, pitch, and roll of the object.

In the research study done at Auburn University and with Adobe, the researchers opted to try coming up with rather convincing looking Adversarial Examples (AX), contriving them to be Outside-of-the-Distribution (OoD) of the training datasets.

For example, using a Photoshop-like technique, they took an image of a yellow school bus and tilted it a few degrees, and went further to conjure up an image of the bus turned on its side. These were made to look like the images in the datasets, including having a background of a road that other school buses in the dataset were also shown upon. This helps to make these adversarial perturbations be focused more so on the object of interest, the school bus in this case, and not have the ANN or DNN hopefully be getting distracted by the background of the image as a giveaway.

To the human eye, these adversarial changes are blatantly obvious.

There wasn't an effort to hide the perturbations by infusing them at a pixel level. You can look at a picture and immediately discern that there is a school bus in the picture, though you might certainly wonder why the school bus is at a tilt. It wasn't bizarre pe se in that some of the reoriented images were plausible. A yellow school bus laying on its side, on a road, well, it could have gotten into an accident and ended-up in that position.

Some of the images might be questioned, like a fire truck that seems to be flying in the air, but I would also bet that if you had a fire truck that went off a bridge or a ramp, you'd be able to get the same kind of reorientation.

For the school bus, some of the reorientations caused the ANN or DNN to report that it was a garbage truck, or that it was a punching bag, or that it was a snowplow. The punching bag classification seems to make sense in that the yellow bus was dangling as though it was being held by its tailpipe, and since it is yellow, it might seem characteristic of a yellow punching bag that is hanging from a ceiling and ready to be punched. I don't know for sure that this is the criteria used by the ANN or DNN, but it seems like a reasonable guess as based on the misclassification.

Of the objects that they decided to convert from their normal or canonical poses in the images, and reoriented to a different pose stance, they were able to get the selected DNN's to do a misclassification 97% of the time.

You might assume that this only happens when the pose is radically altered. You'd be wrong. They tried various pose changes and seemed to find that with just an approximate 10% yaw change, an 8% pitch change, or a 9% roll change, it was enough to fool the DNN.

You might also be thinking that this reorientation only causes a misclassification about school buses, and maybe it doesn't apply to other kinds of objects. Objects they studied included a school bus, park bench, bald eagle, beach wagon, tiger cat, German shepherd, motor scooter, jean, street sign, moving van, umbrella, police van, and a trailer truck.

That's enough of a variety that I think we can reasonably suggest that it showcases a diversity of objects and therefore is generalizable as a potential concern.

Variant Poses Suggest Ultra-Brittleness

Many people refer to today's Machine Learning and Deep Learning as brittle. I'll go even further and claim that it is ultra-brittle. I do so to emphasize the dangers we face by today's ANN and DNN applications. Not only are they brittle with respect to the feature's detection of objects, such as a bright yellow versus a faded yellow, they are brittle when you simply rotate or reorient an object. That's why I am going to call this as being ultra-brittle.

If today's ANN and DNN could deal with most rotations and reorientations, being able to still do a decent job of classifying objects, and they were only confounded by extraordinary poses, I would likely backdown from saying they were ultra-brittle and settle on brittle. The part that catches your attention and your throat is that it doesn't take much of a perturbation to get the usual ANN or DNN to do a misclassification.

In the real-world, when an AI self-driving car is zooming along at 80 miles per hour, you certainly don't want the on-board AI and ANN or DNN to misclassify objects due to their orientation.

I remember one harrowing time that I was driving my car and another car, going in the opposing direction, came across a tilted median that was intended to protect the separated directions of traffic. The car was on an upper street and I was on a lower street.

I don't know whether the driver was drunk or maybe had fallen asleep, but in any case, he dove down toward the lower street. His car was at quite an obtuse angle.

What would an AI self-driving car have determined? Suppose the sensors detected the object but somehow gave it a more harmless classification such as naming it a wild animal, or a tumble weed? If so, the AI action planner might decide that there is no overt threat and not try to guide the self-driving car away, and instead assume that it would be safer to proceed ahead and ram the object, like ramming a deer that has suddenly appeared in the roadway.

I realize that some might shirk off the orientation aspects by suggesting that you are rarely going to see a school bus at an odd angle, or a fire truck, or anything else. I'm not so convinced. If we tried to come up with examples of reoriented objects in real-world settings, I'm betting we could readily identify numerous realistic situations. And, if we are going to ultimately have millions of AI self-driving cars on the roadways, the odds of that many self-driving cars eventually encountering "odd" poses is going to be relatively high.

What To Do About the Poses Problem

There are several ways we can gradually deal with this issue of the poses problem.

They include:

- Improve the ANN or DNN algorithms being used

- Increasing the scale of the ANN or DNN used

- Ensure that the datasets include variant poses

- Use adversarial techniques to ferret out and then mitigate poses issues

- Improve ANN or DNN explanatory capabilities

- Other

Researchers should be trying to devise Deep Learning and Machine Learning algorithms that can semi-automatically try to cope with the poses problem. This might involve the ANN or DNN itself opting to rotate or reorient objects, even though the reorientation wasn't fed into the ANN or DNN via the training dataset. You might liken this to how humans in our minds seem to be able to do rotations of objects, even though we might not have the object in front of us in a rotated position.

If you think that the solution should focus more so on the dataset rather than the ANN or DNN itself, presumably we can try to include more variants of poses of objects into a dataset.

This is not straightforward, unfortunately.

It seems fair to assume that you are not likely to get actual pictures of those objects in a variety of orientations, naturally, and so you'd have to synthesize it. The synthesis itself will need to be convincing, else the images will be tagged by the ANN or DNN simply due to some other factor, akin to my example earlier about the grainy nature of the military equipment images.

Also, keep in mind that you need enough of the reoriented object images to make a difference when the ANN or DNN is doing the training on the dataset. If you have a million pictures of a school bus in a right-side up pose and have a handful of the bus in a tilted posture, the odds are that the pattern matching is going to overlook or ignore or cast aside as noise the tilted postures. This takes us back to the one-shot learning problem too.

You could be tempted to suggest that the dataset maybe should have many of the tilted poses, perhaps more so than the number of poses in a right-side up position. Well, this could be undesirable too. The pattern matching might become reliant on the tilted postures and not be able to recognize sufficiently when the object is in its normal or canonical position.

Darned if you do, darned if you don't.

The Key 4 A's of Datasets for Deep Learning

When we put together our datasets, we tend to think of the mixture in the following way:

- Anticipated poses

- Adaptation poses

- Aberration poses

- Adversarial poses

It's the 4 A's of poses or orientations.

We want to have some portion of the dataset with the anticipated poses, which are usually the right-side up or canonical orientations.

We want to have some portion of the dataset with the adaptation poses, namely postures that you could reasonably expect to occur from time-to-time in the real-world. It's not the norm, but nor is it something that is extraordinary or unheard of in terms of orientation.

We want to ensure that there are a sufficient number of aberrations poses, entailing orientations that are quite rare and seemingly unlikely.

And we want to have some inclusion of adversarial poses that are let's say concocted and would not seem to ever happen naturally, but for which we want to use so that if someone is determined to attack the ANN or DNN, it has already encountered those orientations. Note this is not the pixel-level kind of attacks preparation, which is handled in other ways.

You need to be reviewing your datasets to ascertain what mix you have of the 4 A's. Is it appropriate for what you are trying to achieve with your ANN or DNN? Does the ANN or DNN have enough sensitivity to pick-up on the variants? And so on.

Conclusion

When I was a child, I went to an amusement park that had one of those mirrored mazes, and it included some mirrors that were able to cause you to see things upside down. I remember how I stumbled through the maze, quite disoriented.

A buddy of mine went into it over and over, spending all of his allowance to go repeatedly into the mirror maze. He eventually could not only walk through the maze without any difficulty, he could run throughout the maze and not collide or trip at all. His repeated "training" allowed him to eventually master the reorientation dissonance.

It seems that we need to try and make sure that today's Machine Learning and Deep Learning gets beyond the existing ultra-brittleness, especially regarding the poses or orientation of objects. For most people, they would be dumbfounded to find out that the AI system can be readily fooled or confused by merely reorienting or tilting an object.

Those of us in AI know that the so-called "object recognition" that today's ANN and DNN are doing is not anything close to what humans are able to do in terms of object recognition.

Contemporary automated systems are still rudimentary. This could be an impediment to the advent of AI self-driving cars. Would we want AI self-driving cars to be on our roadways and yet their AI can become intentionally or unintentionally muddled about a driving situation due to the orientation of nearby objects? I think that's not going to fly. The objects orientation poses problem is real and needs to be dealt with for real-world applications.

CHAPTER 3
HUMAN IN-THE-LOOP
AND
AI SELF-DRIVING CARS

CHAPTER 3

HUMAN IN-THE-LOOP
AND
AI SELF-DRIVING CARS

The Viking Sky cruise ship is a statuesque vessel that was built in 2017. Unfortunately, it got itself into hot water recently. In March 2019, while operating in the freezing cold waters of the North Sea coast off of Norway, the ship became disabled and a frightful rescue effort took place to lift the passengers to safety via helicopter, at night time, in pitching seas, and for a ship that was carrying 1,373 passengers and crew. Not the kind of adventure that most likely are seeking on such cruises.

Promoted as a comfortable and intimate cruise ship that was designed and built by experienced nautical architects and designers, the beam is about 95 feet in size and the length is about 745 feet. Constructed in modern times, it is a state-of-the-art sea faring ship that has the latest in capabilities and equipment. The desire was to have a ship that could enrich the cruising experience.

What went wrong on this particular voyage?

According to media reports, the preliminary analysis indicates that the ship was relatively low on oil, which normally would not have been an emergency factor per se, but the heaving seas and the sensors on-board the vessel led to an intriguing and design-questioning misadventure.

Turns out that the sea-heaving sloshing around of the oil in the tanks was so significant that the oil-level sensors triggered that the amount of oil was dangerously low, nearly non-existent. If you don't have enough oil, it's like a car engine, namely that without enough oil in your car, the engine cannot have sufficient lubricant and you are at risk of your engine overheating and conking out, along with the possibility of severe damage to your engine that will be costly to repair or replace. It could even cause other damage, possibly even start an internal fire, etc.

The sensors conveyed the dangerously low oil level by signaling the engines to shut-down.

Apparently, this is an automated aspect that involves the on-board sensing system forcing a shut-down of the engines. There is seemingly no human involvement in the process. It is automatic. One presumes that the architects and designers reasoned that if the engine is going to conk-out and be wiped out, presumably when the oil is dangerously low or nearly non-existent, the prudent thing to do is pull-the-plug on the ship's engines. Makes sense, one would assume.

In a grand convergence of bad luck, this engine automatic shut-down happened just as the cruise ship was in the midst of a storm and perchance was not near a port, though it was near to land, but you can't just dock a cruise ship anywhere. The captain decided to put down the anchor to keep the ship from drifting toward the shore and hitting abundant deadly rocks. The anchoring did keep the ship in place, but you can also imagine the corresponding problem it creates, becoming a bobbing cork in heavy seas and now being unable to try and navigate around or over the life-threatening waves.

The good news is that no one was killed and ultimately everyone was saved. The late-night helicopter operation rescued about 479 passengers off the cruise ship. This took time to achieve, and by then the seas had calmed enough to undertake sea going efforts for the rest of rescue instead of the more daunting air rescue approach.

Imagine though the stories you could tell about your cruise. Instead of the rather typical 12-day mundane cruise with picture after picture of scenic skies and the excessive drinking of martinis, the passengers have a shocking "all's well that ends well" tale that will make them the stars of most-harrowing cruise ship vacations.

There are some fascinating lessons to be learned in this story about the Viking Sky.

Keep in mind that a complete investigation has not yet been undertaken (at the time of this writing herein), and so the details are still sketchy. I hope you'll excuse my willingness to interpret what we know now, even though the existing details might either be incomplete or the media might have misstated matters. Nonetheless, I think we can rise above the specifics herein and aim to ferret out potential lessons, whether or not they actually are imbued in this particular event.

Lessons About Humans In-The-Loop vs Out-of-The-Loop

It has been reported that the oil level sensors apparently automatically forced an engine shutdown. There seemed to not be any human involvement at the time in making the decision to do so. You might at first glance assert that there wasn't a need to have any human involvement in this decision, since the right thing to do was indeed to shutdown the engines, doing so before they overheated, conked out on their own, and possibly caused other damages or sparked a fire.

Case closed.

Not so fast!

Remember that the oil level was supposedly relatively low, but not entirely nonexistent. The heaving seas were claimed as sloshing around the oil in the tanks and led the sensors to believe the oil was dangerously low. I'm sure you've done something like this yourself on a smaller scale basis, whereby you sloshed around liquid in a drinking glass, and at one moment the bottom of the drinking glass appeared empty, while moments later the liquid flowed back into the bottom, and the glass was not fully yet empty.

Perhaps there was sufficient amount of oil in the ship's tanks that the engine did not need to be shutdown immediately.

We don't know for sure that the oil level was truly that dangerously low. I realize you can try to argue that the oil sloshing is another kind of problem, and even if the amount of oil was still sufficient, it is conceivable that the sloshing of the oil would make it difficult or hamper the flow of the oil from the tanks to the engine. Gosh, though, you would kind of assume that a ship builder would know about the sloshing possibilities for an ocean-going vessel, wouldn't you?

In any case, let's pretend that the oil was sufficient to keep the engine going, albeit maybe only a brief period of time, nonetheless the possibility of continuing to use the engines for some length of time still existed (we'll assume).

If so, the captain presumably could have further navigated the ship, again only shortly, but it might have made the difference as to where the ship could have gotten to and potentially anchored. The sensors that were setup to automatically cause the engines to shutdown might have shortchanged the chances of the captain taking other evasive action.

Another interesting element is that the captain or other crew members were seemingly not consulted by the ship's systems and instead the whole matter played out by automation alone. As far as we know, the automated system "thought" that the engines were not getting sufficient oil and therefore the automated approach involved shutting down the engines.

Suppose that the captain or crew knew that the sloshing oil was not as bad an oil-level situation as the sensors were reporting. Maybe the humans running the ship could have reasoned that the sensors were falsely being misled by the heaving seas. Those humans perhaps could have countermanded the automated engine shutdown and instead used the engines a little while longer.

Sure, you might argue that those "reasoning" humans might then have overridden the automatic shutdown and kept going too long, leading to the engines running out of oil eventually and then risking the dangers associated with not having done an earlier shutdown. That's a possibility. But it is also possible that the humans could have run the ship just enough to seek a safer spot, and then they themselves might have engaged an engine shutdown.

We really don't yet know whether any of those scenarios could have happened. We also don't know if those scenarios would have led to a better outcome. Admittedly, the approach that took place was in-the-end "successful" in that no passengers or crew were lost in the emergency. It would be pure speculation that any of the other scenarios might have been safer or not.

The fascinating aspect is that this is an illuminating example of the classic Human In-The-Loop (HITL) versus the Human Out-of-The-Loop (HOTL) situation.

Per the media reports, the sensors for the oil-level had been crafted by the architects and designers to automatically force an engine shutdown in the case of insufficient oil. There seemed to be no provision for the Human In-The-Loop aspects. This was a keep the Human Out-of-The-Loop moment, as devised by the creators of the system.

Whenever you design and craft an automated system, you oftentimes wrestle with this tension between whether to have something be a Human In-The-Loop process or whether it should be a Human Out-of-The-Loop approach.

Perhaps the designers in the case of the Viking Sky were convinced that once the oil level got too low, the practical action was to automatically force an engine shutdown. This might have been smart to do and avoid having a Human In-The-Loop, since the human might have taken too long to make the same decision or otherwise endangered the engine and perhaps the entire ship by not taking the seemingly prudent action of immediately doing an engine shutdown.

It is also possible that the architects and designers did not even contemplate having a Human In-The-Loop on this action at all. We assume they probably did conceive of it, and then explicitly ruled out the use of HITL in this type of situation. Of course, maybe while doing the design, no one considered the HITL aspects. They might have merely discussed what to do once the oil level was near kaput, and the obvious answer was to force an engine shutdown.

Did they consider the possibility of sloshing oil that might cause the oil level sensors to misreport how much oil there was actually in the tanks? We don't know. They might have figured this out and decided that if the sloshing was causing the oil level sensors to report that the oil was really low, it was sufficient to merit shutting down the engines. Once again, they might have made a deliberate design choice of not consulting with any humans in such a situation and decided to proceed with an automatic shutdown as the course of action.

That's the difficulty of trying to identify why sometimes an automated system might have taken a particular automated path, namely, we don't know if the human designers and builders reasoned beforehand about the tradeoffs of a HITL versus a HOTL, or whether they didn't think of it, and so the system became a HITL or a HOTL merely by the happenstance of how they did the design. You would need to dig into the throes of how the automated system was designed and built to discern those aspects.

Trying to find out how a particular automated system was designed and developed can be arduous after-the-fact. There might not be documents retained about how things were devised. The documents might be incomplete and lack the details explaining what was considered.

Usually, documentation is primarily about what the resulting system design became, rather than the tradeoffs and alternatives that were earlier considered. This usually is only found by directly speaking with the humans involved in the design efforts, though this is also murky because different people can have different viewpoints about what was considered and what was not considered.

For the moment, I'll leave to the side a slew of other questions that we could ask about the cruise ship tale. Maybe the design stated that the humans should be consulted if an oil level was going to trigger an engine shutdown, but the developers didn't craft it that way, either by their own choice to override that design approach or by inadvertently not paying close attention to the design details. You cannot assume axiomatically that whatever the design stated was what the developers actually built.

One can also wonder what the provision might have been for false sensor readings.

In this case, the sensors were misleading in terms of not being able to apparently discern that the oil was sloshing around, and we might question why this was not considered as a design factor (maybe it was, and the decision was that it might be overly complicated or costly to deal with).

Suppose too that the sensors had some kind hardware faults that caused them to claim the oil was dangerously low, and yet the oil was actually quite full, did the designers consider this possibility, and if so, would they have at that juncture designed the system to do a Human In-The-Loop to verify what the sensors are claiming, or would it still be a HOTL?

My overarching point is that when you are developing automated systems, there needs to be a careful examination of the advantages and disadvantages of a HITL versus a HOTL. This needs to be done at all levels and subsystems. I say this because it is rare that you could reach a conclusion that all of the varied parts of an automated system would entirely be HITL or entirely be HOTL.

The odds are that there will be portions for which a HOTL might be better than a HITL, and portions whereby a HITL might be better than a HOTL.

I mention this too because I know some AI developers that tell me they never trust humans, which means that any system is presumably better off to go the Human Out-of-The-Loop approach than the Human In-The-Loop. That's the attitude, or shall we politely say "perspective" that some AI developers take.

I can sympathize with their viewpoint. Any seasoned developer has had their seemingly perfectly crafted system undermined by a human at one juncture or another. A human dolt stepped into the middle of a system process, interrupted the system, and made a bad choice, making the system look rather stupid. The developer was irked that others assumed the system was the numbskull, when the developer knew that it was the human interloper was the mess-up, not the automation.

When that happens enough times, there are AI developers that become hardened and cynical about any kind of Human In-The-Loop designs. For those developers, the moment you opt to include the Human In-The-Loop, you might as well plant a flag that says big failure about to occur. You might be told by management that it is the way things will be, and so you shrug your shoulders, proceed as ordered, but know in your heart and soul it is a ticking timebomb, waiting to someday explode and backfire on the system.

The problem with this kind of "never" allow a Human In-The-Loop dogmatic view is that you might end-up with an automated system wherein the lack of a human being able to do something can result in untoward results. Perhaps the cruise ship story provides such an illustration (note: I'm not basing my entire logic though on that one story, so be aware that the cruise ship story might or might not be an exemplar, which doesn't impact my point overall about HITL versus HOTL).

I am trying to drive toward the notion that you cannot beforehand normally declare that an automated system is entirely HITL or entirely HOTL. You need to walk through the details and figure out whether there are places that a HITL or HOTL seem to be the best choice. If you can do this and truly rule-out that the Human In-The-Loop is not the appropriate choice, I suppose at that point you can proceed with an entirely HOTL design.

The Perfection Falsehood Rears Its Head

I'll also emphasize that the HITL versus HOTL question is not necessarily cut-and-dry. Many AI developers tend to live in a binary world wherein they want to make everything into a clear cut on-or-off kind of choice. Usually, the HITL versus HOTL involves gray areas, and encompasses doing an ROI (Return on Investment) comparison of the costs and benefits associated with which choice you make. It is not solely quantifiable though. There is judgement involved. It is not a pure numbers or calculus that can determine these choices.

I'd like to bring up to the "perfection" falsehood that sometimes permeates the design of automated systems.

This involves one side of the HITL versus HOTL trying to contend that either the automated system will act perfectly, or that the human will act perfectly. I'd bet that's not going to happen in terms of the real-world is that an automated system can act imperfectly, and a human can also act imperfectly. The perfection argument is a false one that is misleading and often used to suggest an upper hand, though it is a mirage.

Let's use the cruise ship as example, though again it might not be accurate in terms of what actually did happen.

Imagine a bunch of the ship designers sitting around a table during a JAD (Joint Application Development) session and arguing about whether to have the oil level sensors trigger an automatic shutdown of the engine.

One of the louder and more seasoned designers speaks up, doing so in a commanding voice. We know that humans make mistakes, the designer proclaims, and the automation won't make mistakes since it is, well, it is automated, and so the best choice in this case is to cut the human out of the matter.

You see how perfection is used to assert that the HOTL is the right way to go?

This can be used on the other side of the coin too. Erase for the moment the image of that seasoned designer and start the image anew.

Now, consider this. A seasoned designer stands up, looks around the room, and points out that automation can falter or go awry, and the wise approach would be to include the humans into the matter, since they will always know the right decision to be made. Those humans will consider aspects beyond what the system itself knows about and be able to make a reasoned choice far beyond anything that the automation could do.

Once again, we've got a perfection argument going on, in this case for the HITL approach.

We might all agree that humans have a chance at using reasoning and therefore might indeed be able to do a better selection or choice of actions than an automated system, but this also belies the limitations and weaknesses inherent in including Humans In-The-Loop.

Face it, humans are human. Let's use the cruise ship story to showcase this aspect, which I'll do by stretching the story to do so.

Suppose the cruise ship was designed to ask the humans what to do in the situation when the oil level sensors are reporting that the oil level is extremely low. Maybe the captain or crew opt to completely ignore the warning and do nothing, in which case the engine conks out, and perhaps an on-board fire starts, threatening the entire ship. Bad humans.

Or, maybe the captain and crew see the warning and decide they will use the ship for just five more minutes and will then do a manual engine shutdown. Turns out thought they misgauged the situation, and after two minutes, the engine conks out, becomes destroyed due to waiting too long, and even if oil could be provided now to the ship, the engine is completely useless. Bad humans.

The reality is that any automation can falter or fail, and likewise any human or humans can falter or fail.

There isn't this perfection nirvana that is sometimes portrayed as a means to bolster an opinion about how to design or develop an automated system.

Whenever someone tries the perfection argument on me, I try to remain calm, and I gently nudge them away from their perfection mindset.

It can be hard to do. For those that have had human's mess-up, they tend to swing to the automation-only side, and for those that have had automation mess-up, they tend to swing to the Humans In-The-Loop side. The world is not that easy and not so simplistic, though we might wish it to be.

Range of Characteristics Needed For HITL Versus HOTL Debate

An upside for the Human In-The-Loop approach often involves these kinds of characteristics:

- Humans can potentially provide intelligence into the process

- Humans can potentially provide emotion or compassion into the process

- Humans can potentially detect/mitigate runaway automation

- Humans can potentially detect/overcome nonsensical automation

- Humans can potentially shore-up automation gaps

- Humans can potentially provide guidance to automation

- Etc.

Any of those aspects can be a bolstering toward going the HITL route and not going the HOTL path.

I don't want you to leap to any conclusions, and so I've said the word "potentially" in each of the listed items.

Also, again keep in mind that this is not a blanket statement across an entire system and needs to be done at the subsystem levels too.

We also need to consider the characteristics about the downsides for the Human In-The-Loop:

- Humans can make bad choices due to not thinking things through

- Humans can make bad choices due to emotional clouding

- Humans can slow down a process by taking too long to take an action

- Humans can make errors in the actions they take

- Humans can be disrupted in the midst of taking actions

- Humans can freeze-up and fail to take action when needed

- Etc.

You can essentially reverse those same upsides and downsides and use them to do a characteristics listing for the upsides and downsides of the Human Out-of-the Loop too.

There are some additional salient matters involved.

When designing an overall system, you need to be careful about "sneaking" HITL into subsystems that might be rarely used and having the rest of the system act as HOTL.

In essence, if humans involved in the use of a system are lulled into assuming that it is a Human Out-of-The-Loop because of a rarity of experiencing any Human In-The-Loop circumstances in that system, those humans can become complacent or dulled when the moment arises for them to perform as a Human In-The-Loop.

Examples of this are arising in the emergence of AI self-driving cars. Back-up drivers that are being employed to watch over the AI of a self-driving car are likely to assume they don't need to be attentive, which can happen due to long periods of no need for their human intervention.

The Uber self-driving car incident of ramming and killing a wayward pedestrian in Phoenix is an example of how a back-up driver can become complacent.

This also though will happen to everyday human drivers that begin to use Level 3 self-driving cars. The automation that is getting better will ironically tease humans into become less attentive to the driving task, in spite of the aspect that the human driver is considered always on-the-hook and responsible for the driving of the car. It is an easy mental trap to fall into.

You can also have situations whereby you've devised a system to be primarily HITL and then you have a "hidden" HOTL that catches a human operator by surprise.

Some suggest that the Boeing 737 MAX situation might have had this kind of circumstance.

There was an automated subsystem, the MCAS (Maneuvering Characteristics Augmentation System), which was apparently silently kicking into engagement to take over the plane controls when the automation ascertained it was relevant to do so, yet supposedly there was not a noticeable notification to the pilots and/or it was assumed that the pilots would already be aware of this subtle but significant feature.

You might say that the pilots were primarily a Human In-The-Loop situation in terms of flying the plane for most of the time, while the MCAS was more akin to a Human Out-of-The-Loop subsystem that would pop into the flying on rare occasions.

The pilots, being used to being HITL, could become confounded when a subsystem suddenly invokes a Human Out-of-The-Loop approach, especially so since it tended to occur in the midst of a crisis moment of flying a plane, compounding an already likely chaotic and tense situation.

See Figure 1.

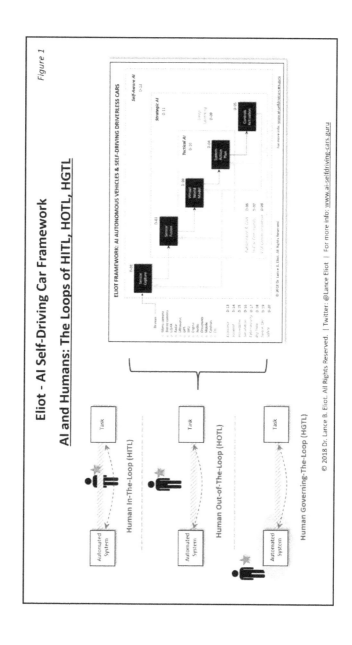

Consider Ramifications of Human Governing-The-Loop

An additional salient element is an aspect that I refer to as the Human Governing-The-Loop or HGTL.

I've so far discussed two sides of the same coin, the Human In-The-Loop and the Human Out-of-The-Loop. We can take a step back somewhat and consider the coin itself, so to speak.

Let's consider the cruise ship again.

Could the captain and crew have potentially turned-off the automated subsystems involved or otherwise prevented the automatic shutdown of the ship's engines?

I don't know if they could have, but let's assume that they probably could have done so. There might have been some kind of master emergency switch that they could have used to turn-off the sensors, presumably preventing the sensors from triggering the engine shutdown. Or, maybe once an engine shutdown is started, perhaps there's an emergency switch that stops the shutdown from proceeding and will keep the engines going.

I'm not saying it would necessarily have been wise for the captain or crew to take such an action. Maybe it would have been much worse to do so. Perhaps turning off the oil sensors might mean they would be blind as to how much oil they really have in the tanks and could cause the captain and crew to run the engine when it should no longer be safely running. And so on.

We can consider instead if you like the Boeing 737 situation.

It appears that the pilots could completely turnoff the MCAS. This could be good or bad. The MCAS was intended to help the pilots and try and prevent a dangerous nose-up situation.

The media has reported that other pilots of the Boeing 737 had from time-to-time opted to turn-off the MCAS and did so to presumably prevent it from intervening and thought that they as human pilots could handle the plane without having the MCAS underway.

My point is that there is often a means for a human to not be per se a Human In-The-Loop and yet still be able to take action as a human that can impact the automated system and the process underway.

They "own" the coin, or at least can overrule the coin in a certain manner of speaking.

If the human can turn-off the automated system, or otherwise govern its activation, I'll call that the Human Governing-The-Loop. I make a distinction between the Human In-The-Loop and the Human Governing-The-Loop by suggesting that the HGTL is not particularly involved necessarily inside the loop of whatever action is taking place. They could be, but they don't have to be.

I might have a factory floor with lots of automated robots. Some of those robots are interacting with humans in a Human In-The-Loop fashion. Some of those robots don't interact with humans at all and are considered entirely Human Out-of-The-Loop.

Suppose a manager of the factory has access to a master switch that can cut power to the entire factory. If they were to smack that master switch, power goes out, and all of the robots come to an abrupt halt. This manager is not actively involved in working with those robots and so is not technically a Human In-The-Loop in the traditional sense.

Yet, the human can do something about the automation, in this case completely halt it. I realize some of you might say if that's the case then the factory manager is indeed a Human In-The-Loop. I don't want to get us bogged down in a debate about this point and concede that you could say that the manager is a Human In-The-Loop, but I dare say it is somewhat misleading due to the omnipresent role that this human has.

For that reason, I have carved out another kind of human loop related role, the Human Governing-The-Loop.

You might not like it, and that's fine. I think it useful though to consider the role and thus tend to call it out and give due attention to it.

There are some systems devised to prevent a human from trying to disable or cut-off the system, which might make sense because it is otherwise a kind of hole or gap related to what the automated system is perhaps intending to do. This might be a security system and just like spy movies you don't want a clever crook to cut-off power and then get access to a treasure trove (spoiler alert, think about the FBI in the movie "Die Hard" and you'll know what I mean by this).

On the other hand, if there is absolutely no means to stop or hinder an automated system, this is the nightmarish predicament you see in many movies that portray an AI system that's gone amok. Some believe that we might be headed to a "singularity" whereby AI becomes all-powerful and there is no means for a human to stop it, i.e., no HGTL.

AI Self-Driving Cars and HITL Versus HOTL

What does this have to do with AI self-driving cars?

At the Cybernetic AI Self-Driving Car Institute, we are developing AI software for self-driving cars. For auto makers and tech firms making AI self-driving cars, the question of HITL versus HOTL is a crucial one. It needs to be explicitly considered and not just be designed or built in a happenstance manner.

Allow me to elaborate.

I'd like to clarify and introduce the notion that there are varying levels of AI self-driving cars. The topmost level is considered Level 5. A Level 5 self-driving car is one that is being driven by the AI and there is no human driver involved. For the design of Level 5 self-driving cars, the auto makers are even removing the gas pedal, brake pedal, and steering wheel, since those are contraptions used by human drivers. The Level 5 self-driving car is not being driven by a human and nor is there an expectation that a human driver will be present in the self-driving car. It's all on the shoulders of the AI to drive the car.

For self-driving cars less than a Level 5, there must be a human driver present in the car. The human driver is currently considered the responsible party for the acts of the car. The AI and the human driver are co-sharing the driving task. In spite of this co-sharing, the human is supposed to remain fully immersed into the driving task and be ready at all times to perform the driving task. I've repeatedly warned about the dangers of this co-sharing arrangement and predicted it will produce many untoward results.

Let's focus herein on the true Level 5 self-driving car. Much of the comments apply to the less than Level 5 self-driving cars too, but the fully autonomous AI self-driving car will receive the most attention in this discussion.

Here's the usual steps involved in the AI driving task:

- Sensor data collection and interpretation

- Sensor fusion

- Virtual world model updating

- AI action planning

- Car controls command issuance

Another key aspect of AI self-driving cars is that they will be driving on our roadways in the midst of human driven cars too.

There are some pundits of AI self-driving cars that continually refer to a utopian world in which there are only AI self-driving cars on the public roads. Currently there are about 250+ million conventional cars in the United States alone, and those cars are not going to magically disappear or become true Level 5 AI self-driving cars overnight.

Indeed, the use of human driven cars will last for many years, likely many decades, and the advent of AI self-driving cars will occur while there are still human driven cars on the roads. This is a crucial point since this means that the AI of self-driving cars needs to be able to contend with not just other AI self-driving cars, but also contend with human driven cars.

It is easy to envision a simplistic and rather unrealistic world in which all AI self-driving cars are politely interacting with each other and being civil about roadway interactions. That's not what is going to be happening for the foreseeable future. AI self-driving cars and human driven cars will need to be able to cope with each other.

Returning to the topic of Human In-The-Loop versus Human Outside-The-Loop, let's consider how this applies to AI self-driving cars, of which I've already provided a glimpse by discussing the role of the human back-up drivers, and furthermore when I discussed the emergence of Level 3 self-driving cars.

HITL and HOTL for Level 4 and Level 3

For self-driving cars less than Level 4, there must be a Human In-The-Loop design since by definition those are cars that involve co-sharing the driving task with a human licensed driver. As a reminder, this then entails figuring out where it makes sense to best use HITL versus HOTL. In other words, not every aspects of the AI for the self-driving car will be using HITL and nor using exclusively HOTL, and instead it will vary.

Keep in mind too that there should be an explicit effort involved in deciding where HITL and HOTL belong. This should not be done by happenstance.

It might also be prudent to document how such decisions were made. Some would say that it will be important later on, in case questions are raised from a product liability perspective. Others might argue that perhaps it might be prudent to not have such documentation, under the belief that it might be used against a firm and undermine their case. Perhaps the standard answer is to consult with your attorney on such matters.

From a regulatory perspective, some of the HITL versus HOTL can pertain to abiding by regulations about the design and development of self-driving cars. Once again this highlights the importance of doing such design by purposeful manner, otherwise the AI self-driving car might run afoul of federal, state or local laws.

We have found it useful to put together a matrix of the various functions and subfunctions of the AI system and then indicate for each element whether it is intended to be HITL or HOTL. Included in this matrix would be an explanation of the rationale for which choice is being made. The matrix tends to change over time as the AI self-driving system is evolving and maturing.

In many cases, a feature or functions starts off as a Human In-The-Loop, doing so because the AI is not yet advanced enough to remove the human from having to be in the loop. Given advances in Machine Learning and Deep Learning, gradually there are driving tasks that shift from being in the hands of the human driver and instead by the "hands" of the AI system.

A number of the auto makers and tech firms are trying to evolve their way from a Level 3 to a Level 4, and then from a Level 4 to a Level 5. Thus, you might have a matrix with a lot of HITL's that gradually become HOTL's. Once you arrive at a Level 5, in theory the matrix is nearly all HOTL's, though I'll provide some caveats about that notion in a moment.

The Level 4 is a bit of a different animal because it relies upon being able to do presumably pure self-driving when within some set of stated ODD's (Operational Design Domains). For example, a Level 4 might state that the AI is able to drive the self-driving car in sunny weather, in a geofenced area, and not at nighttime. When the particular ODD is exceeded, such as in inclement weather or at night time, in this example, the AI is supposed to either bring the self-driving car to a considered safe halt or turn over the driving task to a human.

If the human opts to then takeover the driving once the ODD is exceeded, you are back to essentially a Level 3 situation in that the human driver and the AI are potentially co-sharing the driving task. It seems unlikely that the Level 4 would simply drop down into a Level 2 mode once the AI for the Level 4 is outside of its defined ODD, and more likely that the Level 4 would be essentially the (former) Level 3 that was enhanced to become a Level 4.

As per my earlier remarks, the AI developers need to consider carefully when the HITL will come to play and when the HOTL will come to play, including be cautious about any "hidden" HITL's or HOTL's that rarely are intended to occur.

Some mistakenly believe that only when a HITL is going to occur do you need to alert the human, but I would argue that the same notion of a forewarning or alert should be done when the HOTL is going to happen too.

A rule-of-thumb generally is that no surprises by either a HITL or a HOTL is going to go more smoothly than a sudden surprise instance of a HITL or a HOTL.

HITL and HOTL for Level 5 Self-Driving Cars

For Level 5 self-driving cars, presumably there isn't any Human In-The-Loop involved, due to the notion that the AI is supposed to be able to drive the self-driving car without any human driving assistance.

The Level 5 self-driving car might not have any humans inside the car at all and be driving to say get to a destination to pick-up passengers.

I mention this to point out that there might not be any humans inside a Level 5 self-driving car, which would imply by default that there is no chance to involve a human into the loop even if the AI wanted to do so.

There are various caveats that are worth mentioning, and for which I've often noticed pundits seem to leave out or are not considering.

First, there are some AI self-driving car designers that are opting to include a provision for remote operation of the self-driving car. The idea is that there might times at which you want a remote human driver to take over the wheel. I've previously written and spoken about the aspect that this can be harder to arrange than you think, and in some sense it would imply that the self-driving car is not truly a Level 5 (since it seems to be reliant potentially on a human driver, regardless of whether the human happens to be inside the car or not).

If there is a provision for a remote human operator, this obviously then dictates a Human In-The-Loop need for some amount of the functioning of the AI self-driving car. The same comments about the HITL and HOTL for the Level 4 and Level 3 are equally applicable to a Level 5 that has a remote human operator that can become involved in the driving task.

Another factor about the possibility of a Human In-The-Loop for a Level 5 involves the use of means of electronic communication with a self-driving car. If the Level 5 is using V2V (vehicle-to-vehicle) electronic communications, or possibly V2I (vehicle-to-infrastructure), or possibly V2P (vehicle-to-pedestrian), these are all avenues that might encompass a human. We tend to assume that the V2V and V2I is being provided by another automated system, but that's not necessarily the case. The V2V, V2I, and V2P can be arising from a human (I realize too that you could make the same case for the OTA, Over-The-Air capabilities).

That being said, you might argue that all of these electronic communications are not within the realm of the driving task of the self-driving car and therefore not particularly a valid kind of HITL. They are presumably advisory messages or communiques, and it is up to the AI of the self-driving car to decide what to do about those messages. The AI might use the messages in determining what driving it should do, or it might reject or opt to ignore the messages.

This dovetails into a similar kind of dilemma, namely the situation of having passengers inside the Level 5 self-driving car and what their role might be related to the driving task.

Let's suppose that the Level 5 self-driving car has no actual driving controls for any human use. This implies that a human inside the Level 5 will be unable to do any of the driving, even if they wanted to do so. There is though a kind of way in which the passenger can impact (possibly) the driving the self-driving car, doing so via interaction with the AI system.

You are inside an AI self-driving car. You tell it where you want to go. As the AI proceeds to drive to the destination, you yell at the AI to hit the brakes because you have noticed a dog chasing a cat and those two will cross the path of the self-driving car. The self-driving car has not yet detected those two animals, perhaps because they are both low to the ground and off to the side of the road, though the human passenger saw them and deduced that they are likely to enter into the street.

Are you involved in the driving of the self-driving car?

In this case, we're assuming you aren't in direct control in terms of having access to a steering wheel or the pedals. But, does your verbal command become a different kind of driving control, not one in which you are using your hands or feet to control the car, and instead you are using your voice. Is your voice really that much different than having a physical access to the driving controls?

The point being that a human is presumably going to be in the loop for Level 5 self-driving cars, either by being a passenger and offering driving "commands" to the AI, which might or might not comply, or driving "suggestions" (or directives) might arise via V2X (which encompasses all of the various V2V, V2I, V2P, etc.).

To me, this means that for true AI self-driving cars of a Level 5, you still need to take into account the Human In-The-Loop. It won't be a Human Out-of-The-Loop, at least not entirely, though there are certainly situations in which there isn't any HITL involved.

HGTL and Level 5 Self-Driving Cars

I'd like to bring up the other facet of HITL and HOTL, the HGTL element. I had mentioned that a human might not necessarily be in the loop and yet still have sway over an automated system, doing so in a kind of governance manner, thus the Human Governing-The-Loop.

In theory, if you, a human, do not turn-on your Level 5 AI self-driving car, it's not going to do anything at all. Not everyone agrees with that concept. Some believe that the Level 5 will always be turned on, similar in a manner that you might have Alexa or Siri always on, waiting for an indication from the human that an action of some kind should be undertaken.

Does this mean that you could never fully turn-off your Level 5 AI self-driving car? There must be some means to get it to conk out. Perhaps you would need to reach under-the-hood and disconnect the batteries, denying any power to the self-driving car. That's a bit extreme, it would seem.

Some have suggested that there should be a "kill switch" included inside of the AI self-driving car. One thought is that if you hit the kill switch, it disengages the AI and you now have a self-driving car with nothing able to drive it.

For a Level 5, if there aren't any driving controls physically inside the self-driving car, and if you've turned-off the AI such that the self-driving car won't respond to your voice commands, it would seem like you have quite a hefty paperweight.

I'm bringing this up to mention that we need to be considering the HGTL facets of AI self-driving cars.

It might not seem important right now, due to the aspect that the auto makers and tech firms are mainly trying to get an AI self-driving car that can drive reasonably safely via the AI, but it is a matter that we'll ultimately need to wrestle with.

Conclusion

AI systems tend to aim toward getting Humans Out-of-The-Loop, doing so by leveraging AI capabilities that mimic or attempt to perform in the way that humans do. We cannot rush that direction and end-up falsely believing that an AI system can indeed perform without a HITL when it perhaps cannot realistically do so.

At the same time, if there is a HITL that is being devised, the AI needs to be built in a manner to appropriately interact and co-share with the human. Less surprises are a handy mantra. The same mantra applies to those hidden instances of HOTL.

Besides the classic HITL and HOTL, a slightly more macroscopic viewpoint includes the HGTL.

Even if a human is not directly involved in the automated system and the performance of the scoped tasks, there is likely a governing role that a human can potentially undertake.

Whether this is governing possibility a HITL or not, the HGTL is nonetheless a reminder of identifying what to do about humans that are seemingly not in the loop and nor per se outside of the loop (depending upon the definition of the loop), and yet can nonetheless impact the loop.

There are all kinds of loops, including lopsided ones, reinforcing ones, and loops that either rely upon humans or do not do so. AI systems are going to bring to the forefront the human role inside and outside of loops, doing so in ways that were not as feasible with prior automation. That's my feedback loop to those making AI self-driving cars.

CHAPTER 4

GENIUS SHORTAGE
AND
AI SELF-DRIVING CARS

.

CHAPTER 4

GENIUS SHORTAGE

AND

AI SELF-DRIVING CARS

Is there a genius shortage that is impeding the progress of AI?

This is a pointed question that keeps coming up in the hallways of AI conferences and that people are whispering about. Sure, there has been some impressive efforts of newer AI systems that suggest we are making solid progress in AI, but it's not particularly breakthrough-like improvements that have rocketed AI ahead and overcome some of the as-yet-solved thorny problems in AI.

I had one AI developer that took umbrage at the assertion that there is a genius shortage and insisted that they are a genius and the question itself seemed to undercut his prowess. I politely noted that the question does not say there aren't any geniuses, only that there seems to be a shortage of them. I suppose then that if he wants to believe that he is a genius, he can do so, and the question still remains palatable.

Some people react by saying it is a blatantly stupid question. What does being a genius have to do with progress in AI? Do we need to have an Einstein of AI, or a Darwin of AI, or a Leonardo da Vinci of AI, in order to push further ahead on AI? Where does it say that the only means to progress in a field of endeavor is when you have a genius that happens to be in that field?

In essence, you might make the argument that by-and-large the progress in most fields of endeavor has been undertaken by "less than geniuses" that did the hard work and painstaking efforts to make progress. Lots of really smart people can perhaps do the work of those unicorn geniuses. Historians would likely indicate that those of a genius nature are far and few between, and you'd be unlikely to pin substantive progress in endeavors primarily due to those geniuses alone.

This also brings up the elephant in the room, namely what exactly is a genius and how would we know it when we see it. Einstein today is regarded as a genius, yet during his day there were others that thought he was unorthodox and even wrong in his viewpoints and would not have labeled him as a genius. The same can be said about Darwin and most others of the now labeled geniuses of all time.

What Is Genius Anyway

Some say that genius is in the eye of the beholder.

You might see someone do something and remark that the person is a genius, yet others might smirk that the person was not at all a genius and you were fooled or misled or misunderstood and assumed the person was a genius. You might be tempted to use IQ as a measure of genius and suggest that when you have a certain high number of an IQ that you are ergo a genius.

I don't think the IQ test is the most reliable way to try and attest to whether someone is a genius or not. There are undoubtedly many that have top IQ's and yet they do not manifest themselves into a genius category. I think we usually reserve the genius moniker for someone that accomplishes something of a magnitude that we ascribe as being genius level. As such, merely possessing a high IQ is not a sufficient means of joining the genius club. It probably helps to be able knock on the door of the club, but you need to do something with it.

The AI developer that was perturbed at the notion that he might not be considered a genius does bring up another facet of the matter. You might be a genius and yet nobody knows it, or at least nobody knows about you. You might be working in the backrooms and have not done anything that has caught the world's attention. Or, it might be things they are doing now will someday have an incredible impact, but during your lifetime maybe you remain relatively unknown and unheralded, similar to what has sometimes been the case for some of the world's notable geniuses in history.

At the AI lab you work at, right now, look around, and there might be a genius to your left or your right, on their way toward AI genius breakthroughs or perhaps will do so in a few years (or, if you prefer, look in the mirror!). These budding geniuses might be like the moth that will someday emerge as a butterfly, allowing their inner genius to make its way out and astound the world of AI by solving seemingly insolvable problems.

There is also the matter of genius as a sustained trait versus a transitory or eureka kind of flash of brilliance.

Some falsely assume that the infamous E=MC squared was a sudden harkening by Einstein, you might want to read the voluminous accounts of how he made his way towards the now famous equation over many years of efforts. It is said that Edison made thousands of attempts at perfecting the light bulb, which is somewhat of a mischaracterization, but in any case, it demonstrably is the case that he did not wake-up one morning with the solution in his mind out-of-the-blue as a genius flash.

Hindsight and the writing of history can at times bolster the case for someone being considered a genius. We might then fall into the trap of assuming that the genius flavor was the genesis for an amazing insight that others never had. In fact, many times the alleged insight was one that others also had at the time, and for a variety of confluences it turns out that the one person now having fame as a genius gets the glory, though many others were doing similar work at the time.

I've dragged you through the muddied waters so far about what exactly is this genius that some are saying we don't have enough of. Let's set aside the difficulty of defining this kind of genius, for the moment, and concentrate on whether there is a shortage of them.

If you are going to claim that there is a genius shortage, it implies that there is some magical number or desired threshold of geniuses that we are hopeful of attaining. Presumably, there must be an amount of the number of geniuses that you have in mind to be reached, and you are concerned that we don't have enough of those.

Economic Supply and Demand of Geniuses

How many geniuses do we need in AI?

You could ask the same question of any other field of inquiry. How many geniuses does physics need to make abundant progress in physics? How many geniuses does chemistry need? How many geniuses does biology need? And so on?

You can also ask the same of arenas outside of science and engineering. How many geniuses are needed in music, and is there a shortage of them? What about art? What about any of the fine arts? Maybe we don't have enough geniuses anywhere, in any field, and all fields are being held back because of it.

On the other side of the coin, do we have an abundance of geniuses?

If we had too many of them, I suppose we'd know. Perhaps there would be incredible breakthroughs in all fields at all times. This might happen like popcorn kernels that are popping, the breakthroughs would be sizzling and there would be no denying that we have a plethora of geniuses.

It would seem that we probably don't have an abundance of geniuses, which seems perhaps obvious, and we cannot say for sure that we have a shortage, though it is a somewhat compelling argument to lay claim to the aspect that we might or must have a shortage if things aren't progressing faster than they are.

A recent research paper weighs into the genius shortage debate by trying to model the level of societal genius in an economic manner.

Research by Seth Benzell and Erik Brynjolfsson at MIT provides an interesting look at the so-called G factor, an economic parameter associated with genius. Their study entitled "Digital Abundance and Scarce Genius: Implications for Wages, Interest Rates, and Growth" examines genius as a limiting factor in economic growth. They point out that though the advent of our digital world has allowed labor and capital to become more abundant, we are still limited due to the inelastically supplied complement of human genius.

You might be pondering how we as a society can perhaps make more geniuses. If there is a shortage of them, it would seem logical to try and make more of them.

Some would argue that genius is in your blood, it's a DNA thing. You either have that secret sauce of intrinsic genius within you, or you do not. Others would say that it is something we can foster in people, perhaps by the right kind of training or education. It could also be a mixture, namely that you might need to have some innate genius for which it blossoms because of the right kind of training or education. This is the classic nature versus nurture debate.

By considering the matter overall as an economic one, it is a modeling exercise of having an out-of-balance of supply and demand, in geniuses, an otherwise scarce commodity.

We have a demand for more geniuses, seemingly, and our supply is too low. Its time to cultivate those latent geniuses. Find them, spur them on.

Making Geniuses Via AI Is Another Path

There's another path that some AI developers are hoping for.

Maybe we can craft AI that has genius, therefore we won't necessarily need as many genius people or at least not a lot more people to have genius in order to meet the lack of supply of genius. Use digital technology to make geniuses, either by the AI itself being a genius, or perhaps if that cannot be readily done then at least be an aid to boost humans into becoming geniuses.

It is like digging a ditch. If we can give people a shovel, it is an aid that augments their ability to dig the ditch, and therefore they can more readily do the needed digging. Better yet, have the shovel be a digging machine that without the need for a human to touch a shovel, the hole gets dug. For AI, either make AI that has genius capabilities and let it do the needed genius work or provide AI that gets humans into the genius realm that otherwise those humans could not have likely achieved.

For those of you that are into AI, let's face it, the odds of crafting an AI system that has genius is rather unlikely right now, though I realize you might try to argue that examples such as a top-level chess playing AI system that exhibits "genius" in chess, or similar exemplars. I don't think we're reasonably talking about that same kind of limited domain "genius" as being the equivalent of human genius. Nor does it have the fluidity, plasticity, and other characteristics that I think we can reasonably ascribe to human genius.

I'm sure that I'll get some flak email about this point. Some will say that a human genius in physics only has genius typically with respect to physics, and therefore that's also a limited domain. And so on. I'm not going to try and address all of the back-and-forth herein, and just say that it seems a stretch to say that AI of today has genius.

There are many AI related initiatives that hope to spark genius-level performance in humans. These are often AI systems that try to get a human to think creativity, perhaps prodding the human to think outside the box. These AI systems even at times try to get a debate going with the human, forcing the human to mull over a topic in ways they might not have previously. In spite of such AI, we would likely all agree, I assume, the AI is not genuinely carrying on a discussion or debate that a human could, at least not in the sense of "intelligence" of humans.

On the matter of the potential for AI systems geniuses, worried humans are concerned that this might take us down the path of having an AI singularity or a super-intelligence, and for which we as humans might then become their slaves. Or, the AI might decide to wipe us out entirely. Is this merely conspiracy kind of talk? Or, is there merit to the dangers? Something worthy of further debate.

AI Self-Driving Cars and the Genius Shortage Topic

What does this have to do with AI self-driving cars?

At the Cybernetic AI Self-Driving Car Institute, we are developing AI software for self-driving cars. One looming question for the auto makers and tech firms is whether or not there is a need for geniuses to make the advent of true AI self-driving cars become a reality.

Allow me to elaborate.

I'd like to first clarify and introduce the notion that there are varying levels of AI self-driving cars. The topmost level is considered Level 5. A Level 5 self-driving car is one that is being driven by the AI and there is no human driver involved. For the design of Level 5 self-driving cars, the auto makers are even removing the gas pedal, brake pedal, and steering wheel, since those are contraptions used by human drivers.

The Level 5 self-driving car is not being driven by a human and nor is there an expectation that a human driver will be present in the self-driving car. It's all on the shoulders of the AI to drive the car.

For self-driving cars less than a Level 5, there must be a human driver present in the car. The human driver is currently considered the responsible party for the acts of the car. The AI and the human driver are co-sharing the driving task. In spite of this co-sharing, the human is supposed to remain fully immersed into the driving task and be ready at all times to perform the driving task. I've repeatedly warned about the dangers of this co-sharing arrangement and predicted it will produce many untoward results.

Let's focus herein on the true Level 5 self-driving car. Much of the comments apply to the less than Level 5 self-driving cars too, but the fully autonomous AI self-driving car will receive the most attention in this discussion.

Here's the usual steps involved in the AI driving task:

- Sensor data collection and interpretation

- Sensor fusion

- Virtual world model updating

- AI action planning

- Car controls command issuance

Another key aspect of AI self-driving cars is that they will be driving on our roadways in the midst of human driven cars too. There are some pundits of AI self-driving cars that continually refer to a utopian world in which there are only AI self-driving cars on the public roads. Currently there are about 250+ million conventional cars in the United States alone, and those cars are not going to magically disappear or become true Level 5 AI self-driving cars overnight.

Indeed, the use of human driven cars will last for many years, likely many decades, and the advent of AI self-driving cars will occur while there are still human driven cars on the roads. This is a crucial point since this means that the AI of self-driving cars needs to be able to contend with not just other AI self-driving cars, but also contend with human driven cars.

It is easy to envision a simplistic and rather unrealistic world in which all AI self-driving cars are politely interacting with each other and being civil about roadway interactions. That's not what is going to be happening for the foreseeable future. AI self-driving cars and human driven cars will need to be able to cope with each other.

Genius Shortage and Impact on AI Problems

Returning to the topic of a genius shortage in AI, let's consider the nature of AI problems that need to be solved and whether we'll need genius thinkers to solve those problems.

Also, let's cast this into an applied realm by considering how the pace and advent of true Level 5 self-driving cars might be constrained or delayed if there aren't those geniuses involved in self-driving car efforts.

AI of today lacks common-sense reasoning. This severely limits the ways in which we might make use of AI. Humans seem to know that the sky is blue, the road is flat, and other common-sense elements, all of which are essential to their thinking efforts. Though there are bold efforts to try and incorporate common-sense reasoning into AI, it's a long way from arriving at anything close to what humans have.

Some also liken this to Artificial General Intelligence (AGI), namely having a type of AI that applies across domains and is not focused or fixated on a particular domain.

The AI efforts to-date are primarily narrow in their scope. You might have an AI system that looks for cancer in MRI slides, yet that same AI system does nothing else beyond that narrow task. It would be handy to have AI that could work across many domains and be flexible and fluid in doing so, which humans generally are able to do.

For driving a car, there is an ongoing debate about whether or not the AI needs to have AGI. Human drivers do have AGI, therefore if the AI for a self-driving car is trying to drive like a human, presumably the AI needs to have AGI. Others claim that the driving task is narrow, and therefore there isn't a need to have AGI for the self-driving car driving task.

What about common-sense reasoning? Humans use common sense reasoning when they drive a car. You look around the car and can see that there is a dog chasing a cat, and you reason that the dog will continue to chase the cat and might end-up in the street, in front of your car. You know that the dog is not likely going to stop chasing the cat and probably doesn't realize the dangers of going into the street. Same might be said of the cat.

Does an AI self-driving car need to have common-sense reasoning, similar to the kind of common sense that humans have? Some say that the AI does not need overall common-sense and that it can be programmed sufficiently to have similar qualities. They would also argue that with the use of Machine Learning and Deep Learning, the AI will by osmosis end-up with a variant of common sense due to pattern matching into it.

Others worry that AI self-driving cars are not going to have a semblance of common sense, and as a result the AI will get the self-driving car into untoward predicaments. This will likely then lead to injuries or deaths. The injuries or deaths will cause the public and the regulators to want to slow down the pace of AI self-driving car development and fielding. The whole lack of common-sense reasoning might doom the advent of AI self-driving cars to a much longer and slower evolution, some believe.

If we had more geniuses in AI, would we by now have solved the AGI problem?

If we had more geniuses in AI, would we by now have solved the common-sense reasoning problem?

I don't know how we can answer the question, since of course if you define genius as someone that would have solved those AI problems, the answer is that yes, those problems would be solved by now if we had them around.

We also don't know that there is a magic formula that a genius would discover to then solve those AI problems. It certainly seems unlikely that a magic wand will produce a solution. In that sense, it would seem that this is the workhorse kind of genius needed, rather than the instantaneous flash of genius, though it is hard to say because there might be a magic wand and we cannot envision it as yet.

I've written and spoken about the ravenous desire by tech firms and auto makers for AI top talent. These AI rockstars are the hopes and dreams by those firms to find new solutions, faster solutions, more effective solutions. Depending upon what you consider genius, those AI rockstars might be that diamond in the rough.

More Open Problems in AI That Genius Can Tackle

I've so far named two open problems in AI, the need to develop common-sense reasoning, and the desire to have Artificial General Intelligence (AGI). Those are two of the biggies, but there are more such problems hounding us.

Another AI open problem involves the topic of learning. Today's Machine Learning and Deep Learning is actually shallow when compared to human learning.

How can we get Machine Learning or Deep Learning that can do one-shot learning, whereby after experiencing only one or a few examples the AI is able to generalize and learn about a topic or matter? It's a tough problem to solve.

There is the open problem of getting AI to learn-to-learn. We cannot keep setting up AI systems that we, the humans, have done the construction around what the AI will learn. Presumably, we want to get the AI to be able to learn about how it can learn, and then use that learning to do a better job at learning on its own.

Some even suggest that we need to have the AI begin as a kind of child-AI, and let it grow over time, similar to how humans start as babies and become children and become adults. Perhaps that's the only way toward getting AI that is more robust.

Object recognition is another open problem in AI.

Today's AI systems that do object recognition are not doing the same kind of "recognition" that humans do.

When a human sees a dog running toward the street, the human uses the shape and movement of the dog to figure out that it is a dog, and correspondingly has a lot of knowledge about what dogs are and what they do. AI systems are merely labeling the image of a dog that it might be a thing called a dog, and don't have any semblance of what a dog is per se.

Autonomous navigation is another open problem in AI, including advances desired in SLAM (Simultaneous Location and Mapping).

Most AI self-driving cars rely upon a GPS system to enable them to navigate, in addition to object and scene recognition. Suppose though that we didn't have a GPS available or it was conked out, what would the AI self-driving car do then? A human driver can drive a car without a GPS, and so should the AI be able to do for a self-driving car.

Theory of Mind is another interesting and important AI problem.

Humans that interact with other humans will tend toward having a Theory of Mind about the other person, being able to guess what the other person might be thinking about, or what the person might do in a given situation. The AI systems of today do not have much if any of a Theory of Mind embodiment. They aren't "thinking" about the thinking of others. Likewise, for humans, a human interacting with an AI system is unlikely to be able to discern what is in "the mind" of the AI system, which can lead to some dangerous kinds of dissonance.

In the case of AI self-driving cars, when human drivers are driving a car, they are usually anticipating the actions of other drivers. You watch the car ahead of you and can guess that based on their driving behavior, they are a timid driver and therefore you can anticipate other potential driving moves the person will make. Few AI self-driving car efforts are seeking as yet to embody this kind of capability.

Across the Spectrum of AI Self-Driving Car Elements

I'm not going to enumerate all of the open problems in AI, but I've provided some of the more notable ones and hopefully provided you with an indication of where there might be value in adding a "genius" to try and solve those problems.

If you have exceptional AI developers that are gifted, and they are tackling those problems, can you consider them to be geniuses? If they are not quickly solving these arduous problems, does that imply they must not be geniuses? This is all quite a quagmire.

Let's focus instead on the areas in which we need some super thinking to solve, and I'll focus on the AI self-driving cars realm.

All of the open AI problems I've already mentioned herein are obviously applicable to the AI self-driving cars field, and so keep that in mind. Also, I'd dare say that any AI problem in the AI self-driving cars field is likely applicable to AI overall.

I mention this to highlight that you'd be hard pressed to claim that there is something applicable only to AI self-driving cars and could not ultimately be carried over into other AI areas.

Using my framework about AI self-driving cars, let's consider each of the major elements.

The sensors of an AI self-driving car are the key to sensing what is around the self-driving car. Maybe there are new kinds of sensors that nobody has yet even invented or considered, for which a "genius" might come out of the woodwork and create.

Or, maybe the sensors we have today can be vastly improved. Perhaps there are new ways to develop cameras that will radically improve the images or video captured by the sensors on an AI self-driving car. Maybe there are breakthroughs to be had in radar, ultrasonic sensors, LIDAR, and so on. This also would include not just the hardware aspects, but also the software that does the object recognition and interpretation.

We might be lucky to have a "genius" that can vastly improve sensor fusion. The capability of cohesively bringing together the sensory data and make sense of it, well, it's a tough problem. Similarly, the use of virtual world models could use a "genius" to make those more powerful and capable. The same can be said of the AI action planning portion of an AI self-driving car, and likewise for the car controls commands issuance.

There is also the need for AI self-driving cars to be self-aware. A human driver knows that they are driving a car. The human presumably keeps tabs on themselves, realizing when they are getting sleepy or impaired. We need the AI in an AI self-driving car to have a similar kind of self-awareness. It might take a "genius" to get us there.

Conclusion

Do we have a shortage of geniuses in AI? Besides the aspect that you could presumably say the same thing about nearly all other areas of study, let's just say that if we had more geniuses it might be helpful.

Notice that I say that it might be helpful, rather than categorically saying it would absolutely be helpful. We don't know that the geniuses would necessarily be ones that would help us make progress. Suppose there are geniuses that are devious and opt to take us down a bad path? Or, maybe there are geniuses that are trying to do their best, and yet waste our attention on something that won't payoff. Who knows?

We also tend to think of geniuses as being solitary actors. The image we tend to have is someone that otherwise has a strange or unpleasing personality and they work alone, toiling away, coming up with miraculous new ideas and inventions.

This kind of stereotype tends to bely the reality of "geniuses" that work with others in teams, and might themselves not necessarily produce something new, and instead be an inspiration or guide to others that do. There can even be a team of geniuses, though we often assume they won't get along and will all be pushing and pulling at each other to showcase who the real genius is.

If you are a genius, please jump in and help out on solving these thorny AI problems.

If you are not a genius, maybe you can become one, so please make a go of it.

If you are trying to help someone else to become a genius, try not to go too far since making a genius is not a sure thing.

If you are an AI developer seeking to craft AI-genius, good luck to you and aim to ensure it won't wipe out humanity.

There is a famous quote by philosopher Arthur Schopenhauer, "Talent hits the target no one else can hit; genius hits the target that no one else can see" (in his book, "The World as Will and Representation"), which is worth ruminating on.

Maybe I've not even listed the solutions that a genius will come up with, presumably being able to see problems and solutions that the rest of us aren't even yet able to discern. Go for it, geniuses, let's see what you can do.

CHAPTER 5
SALVAGE YARDS
AND
AI SELF-DRIVING CARS

CHAPTER 5

SALVAGE YARDS

AND

AI SELF-DRIVING CARS

My latest rental car that I picked-up at the Chicago O'Hare airport was a treasure trove of information about prior renters. I could readily see data that had been imported into the car's infotainment system that had come from at least six different smartphones. Lots of favored playlists of people that I didn't know, but I now knew their taste in music.

Even scarier for those prior renters was that many of their contacts had also gotten transferred into the on-board systems of the car. Plus, via the built-in GPS tracking, I could see the specific locations and dates/times of where many of these prior travelers had gone while using the rental car. If I had been a nefarious person, it would have been possible to use all of this info in rather untoward ways. In my case, I was just curious to see what others had opted to leave behind.

When you get out of a rental car and drop it off at the airport or other destination, sometimes people leave behind quite a curious set of physical odds and ends.

The lost-and-found at a car rental office will typically have tons of sunglasses, which are a popular leave-behind, and likewise kids' toys are another common leftover. In my own forgetfulness, I had one time left a charger cord and figured it was worth going back to the car rental agency to see if they had retrieved it from the car that I had rented.

The car rental clerk, upon listening to my pleading to find my charger cord, took me to their oversized bin of leftovers, which had a plethora of forgotten items, including surprisingly that there were numerous sets of keys. Keys upon keys, on key chains, on key rings, on carabiners, you name it. Obviously leaving behind your keys is a frequently forgotten item too (one wonders, don't people miss those keys, and don't they then surmise that they must have left their keys in that rental car they checked-in?).

Anyway, the quite helpful clerk let me rummage around in the bin (security lapse?). There were a lot of charger cords. I could not prove for sure which one was mine, since there were many that looked just like mine. In the end, I retrieved one that was the same as mine and went on my merry way. The lesson of seeing the full-to-the-brim bin was to always double-check and then triple-check my rental cars before I turn them in.

Digital Artifacts Leftover in Cars

In a modern world, we leave behind not just physical artifacts but also digital artifacts.

It is easy to pair your smartphone to the infotainment and GPS systems of a rental car. Apparently, a lot of people don't add together two-plus-two and realize that what goes in won't necessarily come out. When you pair your smartphone, depending upon the nature of the settings, you might be allowing the car's on-board systems to slurp-up all kinds of info out of your handy cellphone.

I suppose that there are some people that are unaware of the transfer of data that occurs. They live in their own non-digital world or are just part of the unwashed of the digital realm. For some of them, the smartphone and Bluetooth are already somewhat magical, I suppose.

There are likely other people that know that it happens, yet perhaps assume that it will miraculously be erased for them. Perhaps it's like the Mission Impossible movies and the inputted data will sizzle and disappear after it is done with your travel journey. This transferred data will self-destruct in ten seconds, good luck, Jim.

Certainly, the rental car agency could include as part of their rental car clean-up checklist the step of them resetting and blanking out the on-board systems that might have collected your private info. This added step would be nice for the renting public. You would never need to worry about it again, assuming that the rental agency actually did the erasure properly, and consistently, and without making any errors or omissions.

Admittedly, it would be an extra step for the rental firm, and if you are cost conscious as a rental agency, you might say that the cost of the labor to do this reset operation is going to be significant. I know it might seem trivial as an action and not seemingly labor intensive if the reset is setup as a one-click operation, but when you multiply doing this for the thousands upon thousands of rental cars in a fleet, the labor becomes mind boggling. If it also added "wasted" time to turning around a rental car, this is another downside factor and means that your fleet of cars cannot be as efficiently put back onto the road to earn more rents.

FCC Provides a Warning About Digital Artifacts Leftovers

The Federal Communications Commission (FCC) has tried to forewarn people about the Bluetooth pairing dangers, including saying this: "If you connect your mobile phone to a rental car, the phone's data may get shared with the car. Be sure to unpair your phone from the car and clear any personal data from the car before you return it. Take the same steps when selling a car that has Bluetooth" (this is stated at the FCC's web site:

https://www.fcc.gov/consumers/guides/how-protect-yourself-online).

Note that the FCC warning also mentions the notion of erasing your data when you sell your own personal car.

I'm betting that many people neglect to do so. I know this for a fact because I bought a "previously owned" (let's say it more plainly, "used") car, and it had all sorts of data from the previous owner. What makes this more insidious is that the data covered a multi-year period of time. In the case of a rental car, presumably it would likely have less data, though it also depends upon how much has been retrieved from your smartphone.

I'm sure there are a lot of people though that when selling a car are more likely to think about their smartphone data that's on-board the car. I would guess that it is something that you would be inclined to consider. A rental car is maybe less likely to be on your mind in terms of having paired your smartphone to it. For a car that you owned, you would be much more cognizant about having used the car's on-board systems, it would seem.

Here's an added twist for you, what about when your car gets wrecked and it is hauled off to a salvage yard.

Would you be thinking about the data that you've left in your wrecked car?

Probably not.

What Happens to a Wrecked Car

If you are car has gotten so wrecked that it cannot be repaired, the odds are that you are mentally and physically done with that car. The car is probably disfigured. It looks horrible. Nobody wants to try and deal with their now contorted and bruised car. It is like losing a loved one, in a sense, since we often grow fond of our cars. I am not saying it's the same as a person or a pet, and merely trying to point out that many times we get emotionally attached to our cars.

I did so. One of my first cars was a nifty sports car. I had wanted that car for many years and saved up to buy it. I was pretty happy the day I bought it. Several years later, the car got stolen. I was devastated at first. My prized car was gone. I got angry. How dare thieves steal my car! I wanted revenge. I hoped the police would find the car thieves and, well, let's just say that street justice seemed to be a fine way to deal with them, if you know what I mean.

I was told by the police that the odds were pretty high that the car was stolen by a local gang. The gang would joyride the car until they had enough of the fun or until the car itself was no longer able to run. Apparently, there was a rash of gang initiation rights that involved stealing a car, and my kind of sports car fit the profile of what was needed to get into a gang. Who knew?

After a few days of being despondent and hoping to get my car back, I gradually changed my mind about the matter. I didn't want the car anymore. It had become soiled by the intrusion of the gang, if indeed that's what had occurred. The car would never be the same, even if the gang somehow decided to park it someplace and walk away from it. My emotional attachment to the car became detached.

Amazingly, about ten days after the car had been stolen, I got a call from the police department, my car had been discovered. I went right away to go see it. The police had it at the official police impound. When my eyes saw the wreck that was left of my car, I knew at that moment that I probably should not have come to see it. It looked lifeless. Plus, the gang had driven it until a tire blew, and they kept driving on the rim, and ultimately rammed it into another car. The poor thing was a mangled and nearly unrecognizable variant of my prized sports car.

The gang had apparently zestfully stripped everything out of the interior once they had decided to abandon it. I mean everything was gone. There wasn't much of anything inside leftover, not even the flooring mats and carpets. This sucker was picked clean. Imagine a skeleton of a car, prior to the auto maker putting the guts into it.

Believe it or not, I had never paired my smartphone to the car. I know this seems nuts, but it was just one of those get-around-to-it kinds of things that I had not done. Fortunately, there wasn't any personal info in the car, other than the car registration had been in the glovebox, which was now gone, along with everything else that had been taken.

In discussing the car with the insurance company, they advised that the cost to repair the car would be excessive and recommended that the car be considered totaled. I quickly agreed. As mentioned, I was over the car by now. And, upon seeing it as a now picked over corpse, I could not imagine ever driving it again, in spite of whatever astounding repairs and fix-up that possibly could be undertaken.

That's the last I ever saw of my sports car.

When I gently and hesitantly asked the insurance agent what would happen to the carcass (I'm wasn't exactly sure that I wanted to know), he explained that it would be hauled off to a salvage yard. Some people call them junkyards, others refer to them as scrapyards. A rose by any other name. In the end, my car would be dismantled.

Any usable parts would be potentially resold onto the used parts market, or in some cases the scrapyard hangs onto the parts or to the carcass and allows prospective used-parts buyers to come and pick over the skeletons. There seems to be a thriving market of people needing to fix up cars and wanting to find the original parts that fit to the same brand and model of car that they own. Often these are car collectors.

My insurance agent explained that the cost of buying a new part from an auto maker is likely going to be a lot pricier than getting a used part that was once on a no-longer operating car. Some scrapyards remove the reusable parts and place them into a salvage warehouse, nearly arranged. More often, the scrapyards just pile up the "deceased" cars and allow car part seekers to roam around and find whatever they think they need.

He also explained that the unusable elements could be turned into scrap that can be sold at bulk prices, especially scrap metal. The front windshield was smashed, but the other windows were still intact, and so those could be removed and potentially sold as-is. My front bumper was ripped off the car entirely and the headlights were pretty much goners too. Meanwhile, the taillights seemed to still be workable, along with the mirrors, the exhaust system, and so on.

I decided that perhaps my sports car would make a better life for someone else, doing so by my "donating" them to the salvage yard.

Well, okay, I didn't actually donate the car, I instead got a check from the insurance company that covered the insured value. I just say in my own mind that I donated it, similar to providing donated organs for science. I'd like to imagine that my banged up, destroyed, tainted sports car had become a helpful source of parts that would make others happy.

The insurance agent told me that likely 75% of the average wrecked car can be put to some other use. I really had no idea what would happen to a wrecked car and the idea that it is "recycled" in this manner seemed generally impressive. Better than it all just sitting in a big heap and rotting away for years upon years.

Have you ever had a car that was scrapped?

According to statistics by the federal government, there are about 15 million cars per year in the United States that end-up in a scrapyard. There are an estimated 250 million cars in the United States. Thus, as you can see, only about 6% of the cars in-hand seem to go to scrapyards each year. I apparently am one of the "lucky" few to have it happen to their car. At least I wasn't in the car during a car accident that ultimately might have wrecked the car and gotten it to go to the wrecking year. Having a gang steal it was an "easier" way to have it end-up at a salvage yard.

The Case of AI Self-Driving Cars

What does this have to do with AI self-driving cars?

At the Cybernetic AI Self-Driving Car Institute, we are developing AI software for self-driving cars. One aspect that few of the auto makers or tech firms are considering is what will happen to the data that's on-board an AI self-driving car once the self-driving car ends-up in a salvage yard.

Allow me to elaborate.

I'd like to first clarify and introduce the notion that there are varying levels of AI self-driving cars. The topmost level is considered Level 5. A Level 5 self-driving car is one that is being driven by the AI and there is no human driver involved.

For the design of Level 5 self-driving cars, the auto makers are even removing the gas pedal, brake pedal, and steering wheel, since those are contraptions used by human drivers. The Level 5 self-driving car is not being driven by a human and nor is there an expectation that a human driver will be present in the self-driving car. It's all on the shoulders of the AI to drive the car.

For self-driving cars less than a Level 5, there must be a human driver present in the car. The human driver is currently considered the responsible party for the acts of the car. The AI and the human driver are co-sharing the driving task. In spite of this co-sharing, the human is supposed to remain fully immersed into the driving task and be ready at all times to perform the driving task. I've repeatedly warned about the dangers of this co-sharing arrangement and predicted it will produce many untoward results.

Let's focus herein on the true Level 5 self-driving car. Much of the comments apply to the less than Level 5 self-driving cars too, but the fully autonomous AI self-driving car will receive the most attention in this discussion.

Here's the usual steps involved in the AI driving task:

- Sensor data collection and interpretation
- Sensor fusion
- Virtual world model updating
- AI action planning
- Car controls command issuance

Another key aspect of AI self-driving cars is that they will be driving on our roadways in the midst of human driven cars too. There are some pundits of AI self-driving cars that continually refer to a utopian world in which there are only AI self-driving cars on the public roads. Currently there are about 250+ million conventional cars in the United States alone, and those cars are not going to magically disappear or become true Level 5 AI self-driving cars overnight.

Indeed, the use of human driven cars will last for many years, likely many decades, and the advent of AI self-driving cars will occur while there are still human driven cars on the roads. This is a crucial point since this means that the AI of self-driving cars needs to be able to contend with not just other AI self-driving cars, but also contend with human driven cars. It is easy to envision a simplistic and rather unrealistic world in which all AI self-driving cars are politely interacting with each other and being civil about roadway interactions. That's not what is going to be happening for the foreseeable future. AI self-driving cars and human driven cars will need to be able to cope with each other.

Wrecked AI Self-Driving Cars Are a Data Treasure Trove

Returning to the topic of AI self-driving cars that end-up in a salvage yard, let's consider why this might happen and what makes it different from a conventional car that is hauled into such a resting place.

First, the big reason that an AI self-driving car differs from a conventional car in terms of the salvage yard is that an AI self-driving car is chock full of sensors and computer processors.

A conventional car is likely to have a limited set of sensors, often not nearly as powerful and full-bodied as those that would be used on a true AI self-driving car. And, the computer processors in a true self-driving car need to be top-of-the-line, superfast to handle the AI running aspects, more so than the processors on a conventional car.

I am not saying that today's modern conventional cars don't have some semblance of sensors and processors. Instead, I am pointing out that on a Level 4 or Level 5 self-driving car, the odds are they are a step-up in terms of capabilities, along with often higher costs too, at least when purchased new.

Furthermore, the amount of on-board system memory is likely a lot more than you would have on a conventional car.

This is where the concern really focuses about having your wrecked AI self-driving car towed into a salvage yard. Remember my earlier story about car rentals that are turned-in and the renter has left personal data in the on-board systems? Magnify that kind of leftover info a thousand-fold, and you have the situation we are facing with AI self-driving cars.

An AI self-driving car is likely to have captured video streams that are left intact in the wrecked AI self-driving car. There is a treasure trove of telematic data about the activity of the self-driving car. There could be data that was transmitted back-and-forth via the OTA (Over-The-Air) electronic communications that might have taken place between your self-driving car and the cloud of the auto maker. There could be V2V (vehicle-to-vehicle) electronic communications stored in the on-board systems, involving your self-driving car communicating with other self-driving cars.

All of this then is in addition to whatever you might have placed into the self-driving car via your connected smartphone.

Things get even worse.

If your AI self-driving car has a voice activated Natural Language Processing (NLP) system that allows you to give verbal commands to the self-driving car, those might also be stored in the on-board systems. If the self-driving car is a Level 2 or Level 3, in which you co-shared the driving task, the odds are that there might be captured info about your driving and the driving aspects of the AI system.

Tesla Examples Found by Researchers

Let's consider the Tesla cars.

According to Tesla's owner manual, here's the kind of Telematics info that could be kept on-board the car:

"To improve our vehicles and services for you, we may collect certain telematics data regarding the performance, usage, operation, and condition of your Tesla vehicle, including: vehicle identification number; speed information; odometer readings; battery use management information; battery charging history; electrical system functions; software version information; infotainment system data; safety-related data and camera images (including information regarding the vehicle's SRS systems, braking and acceleration, security, e-brake, and accidents); short video clips of accidents; information regarding the use and operation of Autopilot, Summon, and other features; and other data to assist in identifying issues and analyzing the performance of the vehicle." (source: https://www.tesla.com/about/legal).

Plus, this kind of data too:

"Data about accidents involving your Tesla vehicle (e.g., air bag deployment and other recent sensor data); data about remote services (e.g., remote lock/unlock, start/stop charge, and honk-the-horn commands); a data report to confirm that your vehicle is online together with information about the current software version and certain telematics data; vehicle connectivity information; data about any issues that could materially impair operation of your vehicle; data about any safety-critical issues; and data about each software and firmware update."

In case you are thinking that this is merely an abstract problem and would not occur in the real-world, there is a fascinating study that was recently released about a computer security company that bought some wrecked Tesla cars at a salvage yard and examined those cars to see what they could find (for an article and a video of what they found, see: https://www.cnbc.com/2019/03/29/tesla-model-3-keeps-data-like-crash-videos-location-phone-contacts.html).

The researchers looked into four cars that they obtained, specifically a Tesla Model X, a Tesla Model S, and two of the Tesla Model 3 cars. Of course, they found paired data from smartphones. I'd say that's pretty much to be expected of any modern-day car, and not especially surprising or unusual. This included nearly a dozen phonebooks of contact info, and various GPS navigation locations.

What's more interesting is the aspect that for one of the Model 3's, the researchers extracted the video of the Model 3 of when it had crashed. The car had veered off the road and crashed, which the front cameras recorded. Tying this to the GPS data, the researchers could ascertain the location, Orleans, Massachusetts, occurring on Manequoit Road, and the day and time of the crash. The airbags also deployed. They also tied the crash to the smartphone that was plugged into the car at the time, being able to figure out presumably the person driving the car.

They also looked at the log of the phone use and could see that a phone call from a family member (a contact in the database) had called the driver of the car, moments before the crash occurred.

I think we would all be rather shocked to find out that our private details could be so easily gleaned from our wrecked car. You would normally likely assume that those kinds of details would need to be gotten by a court order or a subpoena of some kind.

Also, you would likely assume that the data would be secured in some manner, making it hard for just anyone to retrieve. According to the researchers, by-and-large the data collected was unencrypted. There was no need to try and crack any difficult ciphers or codes.

I don't want to seemingly be picking on Tesla, and it should be pointed out that the Tesla licensing does have some warnings about a salvaged Tesla, including this:

"An unsupported or salvaged vehicle is a vehicle that has been declared a total loss, commonly after extensive damage caused by a crash, flooding, fire, or similar hazard, and has been (or qualifies to be) registered and/or titled by its owner as a salvaged vehicle or its equivalent pursuant to local jurisdiction or industry practice. Salvage registration/titling typically can never be removed from the vehicle so that all future persons understand the condition and value of the vehicle. Tesla does not warrant the safety or operability of salvaged vehicles. Repairs performed to bring a salvaged vehicle back into service may not meet Tesla standards or specifications and that is why the vehicle is unsupported. Consequently, any failures, damages, or injuries occurring as a result of such repairs or continued operation of an unsupported vehicle are solely the responsibility of the vehicle owner" (source: https://www.tesla.com/about/legal).

In a manner of speaking, presumably it is the duty of the car owner to cope with the matter of having their own car salvaged and taking any needed steps.

According to the researchers, Tesla apparently reported to them that:

"Tesla already offers options that customers can use to protect personal data stored on their car, including a factory reset option for deleting personal data and restoring customized settings to factory defaults, and a Valet Mode for hiding personal data (among other functions) when giving their keys to a valet. That said, we are always committed to finding and improving upon the right balance between technical vehicle needs and the privacy of our customers" (as stated in: https://www.cnbc.com/2019/03/29/tesla-model-3-keeps-data-like-crash-videos-location-phone-contacts.html).

You can interpret the response by Tesla as befits your own views about what responsibility the car maker has versus the car owner.

Coping With AI Self-Driving Cars Once Wrecked

As the advent of AI self-driving cars continues to increase, there will be more and more circumstances involving wrecked AI self-driving cars.

Right now, the Tesla's, which are considered pretty much a Level 2, those are the most prevalent of any semblance of an AI self-driving car and so it is logical that those would be getting wrecked, in the normal course of being on the roads, and end-up in salvage yards.

With the emergence of Level 3's, once those become relatively popular, they will ultimately get into wrecks, sorry to say, but it's a fact, because they are cars, and that's what happens with cars, and so those too will eventually get piled into scrapyards.

The Level 4 and Level 5 self-driving cars are right now working in experimental modes and prove-of-concept (POC) modes, and are not owned by individuals per se. Instead, they are being crafted by auto makers and tech firms. This means those self-driving cars are lovingly tended by a slew of expert mechanics and AI professionals. If those self-driving cars get into a wreck, it isn't as though they will just tow the self-driving cars to the nearest salvage yard and junk them there.

Nope. Those babies lead a pampered life, right now.

My point being that the auto makers and tech firms have not had to deal with the end-of-life aspects as yet of self-driving cars. We are still so much at the start of the life-cycle that thinking about the end of the life cycle is nearly unimaginable. AI developers that I talk with are oft to scoff at the end-of-life of their creations, doing so because they are harried and knee deep into just trying to make AI self-driving cars that work, being able to have the AI drive around without hitting anything or anyone.

You might be tempted to suggest that at least the on-board data should always be encrypted.

By doing so, it would mean that even if the wrecked self-driving car was given to a salvage yard, it would be arduous or perhaps infeasible for anyone to readily pluck the data out of the car in terms of knowing what the data actually contained (they might be able to grab it, but it would appear to be undecipherable).

Though this is a good idea, it also offers the downside of having to be continually encrypting and potentially decrypting data to make use of it to drive the self-driving car by the AI system.

This means that the on-board computer systems are going to do a lot of added computational work. The data being collected by the sensors would need to be turned from plaintext or plain-data into encrypted data. Would this happen only once the data is stored? That's data in-rest or in-place. Would it also occur when the data is flowing throughout the on-board system, which is data-in-motion?

There are lots of questions to be considered. Would the added computational effort dilute the on-board computational processors and distract those processors from the "real work" of running the AI to drive the car? Would the time it takes to encrypt and decrypt create a potential delay in having the AI be able to readily make driving decisions, which are real-time and life-or-death kinds of matters?

Some say that maybe have the data encrypted at the end of a driving day, thus only the data that might so happen to be "live" when a wreck occurs would be potentially unencrypted.

Another suggestion is that the self-driving car should have a "wrecked mode" that would automatically kick-in when the self-driving car gets into a crash of some kind. This would either encrypt the data at that juncture, though you need to hope that the processors and systems are working sufficiently that this could actually occur after the crash has happened, or the wrecked mode might erase everything, similar to my Mission Impossible comment earlier (again, this assumes that the AI is still working sufficiently).

One concern about the erasing of data would be whether the data might be needed for purposes of establishing any legal claims about a crash that has occurred. Whether or not our society would allow the auto makers or tech firms to summarily have a feature that would automatically erase everything, well, that's a pretty big if.

You could say that it is up to the owner of the self-driving car to take proper action with their wrecked car. Thus, if someone is "stupid enough" to handover their wrecked car to a salvage yard, and leave all of their personal data in it, that's their own act of being a dolt.

Some would have more sympathy toward the owner of a wrecked car. Would the owner understand that it is their responsibility to deal with the data? Would they realize that the data was even being collected? Would they realize that it wasn't automatically being encrypted for them? Would they understand that it is something they need to take overt action about?

I think we can likely agree that having something in an owner's manual is not quite the most broadcast way to inform car owners. How many of us actually read the owner's manual? It is akin to those that download and use an app, which has a 50 page online licensing contract, and for which most people just click yes and agree to the terms. If the app then gives up all their personal data and sells it to the dark web, do we merely say that those people were dolts?

It could be that some might argue that the salvage yards have an obligation to not allow the data from the towed-in self-driving cars to be handed out. Perhaps there should be legislation that requires salvage yards to protect your data and inform you about it. I doubt that many salvage yards will welcome such an added burden onto their shoulders.

You might say that it should be on the shoulders of the auto maker and tech firms that make the AI self-driving cars. That's again something that has yet to be ascertained in terms of what the range and nature of their duties are. Much of this is still an open market approach and there is little yet in the way of regulatory rules about it.

I would guess that we'll likely see lawsuits that will also arise due to these matters. Someone that has had a wrecked AI self-driving car that reveals private aspects will launch a lawsuit against the auto maker or tech firm, perhaps at the insurance firm, perhaps at the salvage yard, and maybe at anyone or anything in the life cycle steps after a self-driving car has gotten wrecked.

Things Will Get Worse In Terms of What's On-Board

I'll add more fuel to the fire.

It seems likely that true Level 5 AI self-driving cars will have cameras pointing inward and be recording the audio and video of whatever happens inside of the self-driving car. Why this kind of intrusion? It can be to help the AI figure out what the human passengers are doing and what they want the AI to do for them.

There's another equally practical reason, namely for ridesharing purposes. Most would agree that the AI self-driving car of a Level 5 will be used for ridesharing purposes. Even if you own your own Level 5 self-driving car, you will likely let it roam and be a ridesharing vehicle while you are at work or asleep, allowing your self-driving car to make money for you.

By having the cameras that point inward, you can keep track of those pesky ridesharing passengers that might decide to trash the inside of your shiny AI self-driving car. Or, perhaps it could be that someone is having a heart attack and needs urgent help, which the AI might be able to detect by scanning the interior video and then contacting 911 or routing the self-driving car to the nearest hospital.

The overall point is that this kind of private data would also be presumably kept on-board the self-driving car. Once again, it might be accessed once the self-driving car is relegated to a salvage yard, if not otherwise protected or erased.

I'll scare you about the outward facing cameras too.

As your AI self-driving car goes down the street in your neighborhood, it is capturing video, along with possibility audio, and radar, and LIDAR, and ultrasonic waves, which could be kept on-board the self-driving car. It might be sitting in there, a view of all of your neighbors, their dogs and cats, their comings and goings.

When you park your AI self-driving car in your garage, it might still be recording. This could occur in that the AI self-driving car might be setup to wait for you to ask it to do something, so it is sitting there in a semi-alert fashion. It is akin to Alexa or Siri, listening for a prompting word. Though in theory the listening mode is not recording, you never know how it might really have been established.

Some believe that the AI of the self-driving car will be a kind of therapist, allowing you or your children to interact with it on your daily commute.

The AI might try to help you with that problem at work, or difficulties with your spouse. Or, your children might confide that they are failing in their classes and want to run away from home. All of this potentially could be recorded by the AI system.

This AI would use a mixture of NLP, socio-behavioral techniques, and possibly Machine Learning and Deep Learning. Whatever methods or technologies used, it all depends upon having data, including collecting it and keeping it around, in some manner, whether in whole or in a compressed or selected manner.

We really haven't as yet established what the boundaries are going to be about the recording of such data.

I know some pundits claim that the voluminous data is so voluminous that it would not make any sense for the self-driving car to keep it on-board. The amount of on-board computer memory would be overly costly, use up too much power, and be large and heavy, weighing down the AI self-driving car. They say that this data either won't be kept, or it will be shunted up to the cloud via the OTA.

We'll have to wait and see how this plays out.

Conclusion

If I was sad when my sports car went to the salvage yard, imagine how I might feel when my true Level 5 AI self-driving car (of the future) ends-up there too. My sports car could not interact with me, and yet I considered it my friend. For the Level 5 self-driving car, presumably it will be a friend, a confidant, a father confessor, a butler, and probably know more about me than any other living human being. Yikes!

In any case, we do need to all start considering what to do about AI self-driving cars and the data they are going to be collecting. The focus herein was what happens to the data when the self-driving car gets junked to a salvage yard.

That's just the tip of the iceberg. While the self-driving car is still fully active, we need to be worrying about the data and how it is being collected and who can access it.

The next time you drive past a scrapyard, look at the pile of cars, and think to yourself about the hidden secrets that will someday be there, embedded into the computer memory of those AI self-driving cars that were unceremoniously dumped there. Perhaps we'll prevent that data dumpster treasure trove from happening, if we take heed now in the design and development of AI self-driving cars.

CHAPTER 6

PRECISION SCHEDULING
AND
AI SELF-DRIVING CAR

Lance B. Eliot

CHAPTER 6

PRECISION SCHEDULING

AND

AI SELF-DRIVING CAR

Norfolk Southern Corp is doing a makeover of some rather convoluted trainyards. Turns out there are freight railroads that funnel into hubs that have been run the same way for over a century. Generally, freight trains roll into these hectic hubs, the workhorse trains sit around idly waiting for their cargo, and when things seem to reach a suitable readiness of loaded trains ready to roll, the freight trains then head-out on their treks.

It is reportedly a remarkably ad hoc activity and overseen by a seat-of-the-pants approach (see this article in WSJ https://www.wsj.com/articles/a-revolution-sweeping-railroads-upends-how-america-moves-its-stuff).

The hope by several of the major train firms, acting as freight haulers, will be to transform this seemingly chaotic hub activity into a precision of scheduling and efficiency.

By revamping the freight train operations, there are intentions to make this complicated dance into one that is tightly woven with specific entry and exit times, predicted in-advance, and carefully tracked schedules.

Presumably, this will allow for more freight movement, more timely freight movement, and make better use of the railroad's scarce resources. Think of an airport with the daily and moment-to-moment ballet of planes arriving and departing, doing so based on published schedules, along with sticking to the timetables as much as possible.

The notion of transforming the freight train operations is being referred to as Precision Scheduling Railroading (PSR). In theory, the PSR approach should be able to achieve the desired boosts in efficiency and effectiveness.

Having done quite a number of business process revamps in my working career, I can attest that the theory is often easier than the practical reality. I'm sure that there is a chance that the PSR might at first fail to adequately model the realities of the freight train operations, perhaps leading to worse chaos and poorer efficiencies and effectiveness at the get-go.

It takes a lot of elbow grease to make sure that formerly by-hand efforts are not forsaken as somehow backward and inappropriate. The odds are that those manual methods evolved over many years and includes lots of workarounds that keep the trains rolling. It might not be the most efficient approach, but it gets the job done. There is a chance that a new system could upend that approach and inadvertently foul things up, albeit only initially, once the kinks get ironed out.

This effort also needs to consider the ramifications of upstream and downstream vital touchpoints.

Will the freight train customers be able to accommodate a more measured schedule? Those customers are likely making use of processes and operations that assume the hub has an ad hoc schedule. When the hub changes to a more precise and tenacious schedule, those customers will need to likewise alter how they do their business.

I mention this aspect because sometimes a business process change is narrowly focused and fails to consider the cascading impacts. You might fix the hub, but meanwhile all the feeders into the hub and the feeds out of the hub are entering into a set of processes and systems that won't know what to do with the revamped approach. This will undercut the hub changes and possibly befuddle those that had assumed they would right away witness crucial improvements in efficiencies and effectiveness.

The hub itself has its own constraints too that need to be considered.

Let's assume that there are a set number of tracks, N, and you come up with a schedule that assumes there are N+1 tracks, well, that's going to be a problem for those workers at the hub (not enough tracks to abide by the system produced schedule!).

Or, maybe the scheduling system assumes that all N tracks can be used, but it could be that on some days a given track has problems and needs to be repaired before it can be used, so there are really only N-1 or N-2, etc. available tracks. Does the scheduling system take that kind of contingency into account?

You are going to have some number of trains coming into the hub, a number T. Meanwhile, there are some number of trains trying to exit from the hub, a number X. Can those T coming into the hub do so on that number of tracks N, while at the same time dealing with the X number of trains aiming to get out of the hub on those same tracks N?

In today's modern age, there are lots of excellent scheduling systems that are used for a variety of industries, and can handle these kinds of complexities, thus the train hub is not unique or an impossible operation to come under PSR. The point is that it is not as easy as it might seem at first glance. Switching over from an older set of processes to a new set can be tricky and slamming in a fancy scheduling system is not something you can do overnight.

I'd like to focus your attention on another kind of scheduling problem that will soon become a notable and visible concern. It has to do with the advent of ridesharing.

Ridesharing as a Scheduling Problem

I was recently visiting a company on the east coast that was outside of a downtown area and not especially close to any kind of public transportation. I had been invited to attend a session at the firm that took place each Tuesday and involved a gathering of managers from throughout the firm, all coming to HQ from a variety of places across the United States.

There was a train station that I had been advised would be a handy place for me to arrive at and then use a taxi or ridesharing to get over to the HQ building. I did so. After a full-day of discussions, the Tuesday event ended promptly at 6:30 p.m. The firm prided itself on doing things on-schedule and had made sure that each of the sessions started and ended precisely on-time.

I happened to glance out the window of the HQ at 6:15 p.m. and noticed that cars seemed to be gathering out on the nearby streets. Lots of cars. It almost looked like a flock of birds that were coming to get some leftover food scraps. There was a lot of hustling and bustling going on. Some of the cars were cruising back-and-forth, while others were standing still at curbs, and a few had pulled into actual parking spots.

What was happening?

It turns out that the local ridesharing and taxi services all knew that the HQ had these Tuesday events and that the events ended at precisely 6:30 p.m. As a result, these car services were all vying to be nearby when the exodus of visitors wanted to all head-out.

I rode in one of the ridesharing cars and spoke to the driver. He explained that when the Tuesday meetings first began, only a few of the ridesharing drivers knew about it. They were caught somewhat off-guard and there weren't enough cars arriving in time for the 6:30 p.m. exit, meaning that many of those that wanted to get a ride had to wait. Furthermore, some of the drivers arrived belatedly, getting there at say 7:00 p.m., and the rush of people needing rides had by then dissipated.

Word spread among the ridesharing and taxi services that on Tuesday nights at 6:30 p.m. there would be a swelling of demand for rides at this location. Many of these drivers would normally not have much traffic at that time because the area was outside of a downtown location. This HQ event represented a high potential for fares, including some rides that would be longer and more profitable than doing the usual neighborhood and grocery store kinds of runs.

It was fascinating to witness this somewhat "spontaneous" assembly of ridesharing and taxi services to meet the Tuesday night demand. I could see that not all of the assembled cars were going to get riders. There was no predetermined balancing of supply and demand. The driver of my ridesharing lift told me that the Tuesday night occasions had become overburdened with too many lift cars, making the situation into a cutthroat effort to grab riders.

He explained that the closer that a car could physically get to the HQ building, the higher the odds of getting a rider. But most of the other drivers figured this out too, and so they jockeyed to get close to the building. It became a raw act of trying to outmaneuver other cars and push or shove your way closest to the HQ office.

Some wised up and realize that in a first-to-arrive mode, those ridesharing cars and taxis that got there the soonest were able to secure a spot closest to the building. Gradually, the cars began to arrive sooner and sooner, because of the competitiveness of wanting to get one of those vaunted slots nearest to the building. Eventually, some of the ridesharing and taxi cars were arriving a full hour early, simply to get a vaunted spot next to the exit doors of HQ.

You must have some sympathy for these working stiffs, since my driver pointed out to me that by arriving sooner, you did get a higher chance of getting a fare, but this also meant that you likely were spurning other possible fares that you might have gotten at say 5:30 p.m. or 6:00 p.m., since it would have kept you away from getting to the building early.

Which was better, these drivers must have pondered, not be at the building early enough and therefore possibly get other fares elsewhere and but end-up at the low-end of fare chances at 6:30 p.m. or arrive early to the HQ to essentially guarantee you'd get a fare, and yet be idle and unpaid during that waiting time.

A few weeks later, I came back to one of the Tuesday events and found out that the HQ had decided to step into the car lifts aspects and try to straighten things out.

The HQ had made a deal with one particular ridesharing firm for picking up of the riders at 6:30 p.m., doing so by negotiating a special rate for the riders and turning the otherwise "catch as catch can" into a more rigorous process. This meant that the other ridesharing firms and taxi services now realized that at best they might get some leftover crumbs and so they opted to no longer come over to the HQ to try and get riders.

Interestingly, the problem now for some of the riders was that there weren't enough cars available to satisfy the demand.

My guess was that the HQ would be talking with the ridesharing firm about ensuring that enough cars would show-up to meet the demand. The lower price of the fares was handy, yet there was also the need to make sure there were enough cars to provide lifts, and not let the wait time get out-of-hand.

This was especially the case since the Tuesday visitors were used to the idea that there would be an overwhelming number of cars and the odds of instantly getting a lift had been extremely high, prior to the switchover to a specific ridesharing firm. The old way of doing things seemed to have led to a tremendous amount of supply of cars and the riders had the upper hand. Now, in this more reasoned approach, the riders seemed to be less catered to. I'm sure that the next time I go to the Tuesday event, those kinks will have been likely worked out.

I hope you can see that this story is yet another example of a type of scheduling problem.

Similar to the freight trains, there are a multitude of needs for transport in this ridesharing example, and a need to figure out the balance of supply and demand.

You might be able to leave things to a Darwinian approach of letting nature kind of work things out, akin to what happened at first with the ridesharing and taxi firms that wanted to serve the riders at HQ, and what has seemingly occurred at the freight train hubs.

Unfortunately, the ad hoc method can be a hit-or-miss and instead, presumably, a well-design and well-implemented approach is likely to produce better results, once it has been put in place and tweaked accordingly.

AI Self-Driving Cars and Ridesharing Aspects

What does this have to do with AI self-driving cars?

At the Cybernetic AI Self-Driving Car Institute, we are developing AI software for self-driving cars. Most pundits predict that AI self-driving cars will be used as ridesharing cars, doing so to recoup their cost and earn some added dough by fully utilizing the self-driving cars. This will likely lead to some hefty scheduling issues.

Allow me to elaborate.

I'd like to first clarify and introduce the notion that there are varying levels of AI self-driving cars. The topmost level is considered Level 5. A Level 5 self-driving car is one that is being driven by the AI and there is no human driver involved. For the design of Level 5 self-driving cars, the auto makers are even removing the gas pedal, brake pedal, and steering wheel, since those are contraptions used by human drivers. The Level 5 self-driving car is not being driven by a human and nor is there an expectation that a human driver will be present in the self-driving car. It's all on the shoulders of the AI to drive the car.

For self-driving cars less than a Level 5, there must be a human driver present in the car. The human driver is currently considered the responsible party for the acts of the car. The AI and the human driver are co-sharing the driving task. In spite of this co-sharing, the human is supposed to remain fully immersed into the driving task and be ready at all times to perform the driving task. I've repeatedly warned about the dangers of this co-sharing arrangement and predicted it will produce many untoward results.

Let's focus herein on the true Level 5 self-driving car. Much of the comments apply to the less than Level 5 self-driving cars too, but the fully autonomous AI self-driving car will receive the most attention in this discussion.

Here's the usual steps involved in the AI driving task:

- Sensor data collection and interpretation

- Sensor fusion

- Virtual world model updating

- AI action planning

- Car controls command issuance

Another key aspect of AI self-driving cars is that they will be driving on our roadways in the midst of human driven cars too. There are some pundits of AI self-driving cars that continually refer to a utopian world in which there are only AI self-driving cars on the public roads. Currently there are about 250+ million conventional cars in the United States alone, and those cars are not going to magically disappear or become true Level 5 AI self-driving cars overnight.

Indeed, the use of human driven cars will last for many years, likely many decades, and the advent of AI self-driving cars will occur while there are still human driven cars on the roads. This is a crucial point since this means that the AI of self-driving cars needs to be able to contend with not just other AI self-driving cars, but also contend with human driven cars.

It is easy to envision a simplistic and rather unrealistic world in which all AI self-driving cars are politely interacting with each other and being civil about roadway interactions. That's not what is going to be happening for the foreseeable future. AI self-driving cars and human driven cars will need to be able to cope with each other.

Returning to the topic of AI self-driving cars and ridesharing, along with the topic of scheduling, let's consider what the future is likely to present.

I've stated in my writings and speeches that the advent of AI self-driving cars will be more so than solely being done as fleets.

As background for you, some pundits claim that no one will individually own an AI self-driving car because such vehicles will be overly expensive. Therefore, in this theory, AI self-driving cars will be owned by the likes of either auto makers, tech firms, or ridesharing firms, and be considered as working in collectives that we might call a fleet of AI self-driving cars.

That seems like a rather narrow view of the future.

AI Self-Driving Cars to Become a Flood of Ridesharing

If an auto maker or tech firm or ridesharing firm can make a buck off of AI self-driving cars, why wouldn't individuals seek to do the same?

Those with this other theory are narrow thinking in that they view car ownership as simply and exclusively a cost. Today, when you buy a car, you use it to go to work, and going on vacation, and driving to the store, etc. You aren't making money by owning the car. It is your means of conveniently getting around.

The advantage of an AI self-driving car is that it comes with a built-in driver (in the case of true Level 5 AI self-driving cars). This means that the AI self-driving car can be used whenever you want, and you don't need to be the driver, and nor do you need to find or hire a driver. Keeping in mind too that most people only use their car for about 5-10% of the day, a car is a tremendously underutilized asset that can be deployed to your personal and financial wellbeing.

How could you afford an AI self-driving car if it might cost into the hundreds of thousands of dollars? Easy, by turning it into a money maker. While you are at work, you send your AI self-driving car out to do ridesharing. When you are asleep, you do likewise.

This will create a huge cottage industry of small onesie type businesses, whereby you purposely buy an AI self-driving car, likely taking out a loan to cover it, and are anticipating that the revenue generated by the AI self-driving car will make your purchase worthwhile. There is a chance of a solid ROI (Return On Investment) for this approach of buying an expensive asset and putting it to work.

I'm predicting, perhaps boldly, we'll see a flourishing cottage industry surrounding the advent of AI self-driving cars.

That being said, I've also forewarned that this blossoming might get somewhat out-of-hand.

Besides individuals jumping into the fray, and besides the usual suspects like ridesharing firms and auto makers, you might as well add other kinds of firms too. You could be a firm in a completely unrelated industry and see the writing on the wall that money can be made off the backs of AI self-driving cars.

Today's firms that make money from the utilization of cars for ridesharing have to jump through lots of hoops to do so. Ridesharing firms need to find drivers and keep those drivers happy. No need to do so for an AI system that's your always available driver, it's happy already (well, kind of). You can also readily outsource things like the maintenance needed for the self-driving cars and other kinds of logistics aspects.

If my predictions come true, we'll see a flood of AI self-driving cars that are flowing in and around our streets. This will be the next gold rush.

Let's consider then the notion of AI self-driving cars roaming around our streets.

Pundits tend to imagine a Utopian world in which you come out to the street and within seconds there is an AI self-driving car there at your beck and call. Sounds great! We will all be able to reduce delay time in getting a ride. Rides on demand.

Yes, that might be true, but how did that AI self-driving car get to you, doing so quickly?

You might have requested it in-advance, perhaps via a mobile app, and then when it arrived, you went outside to get into it for your ride. That's one way to arrange the ride.

Another involves simply going out to the curb and hailing a ride. I'd dare say most of us are using that method these days. You used to hail a cab by waving frantically at cabs that wandered past you. Now, you use your mobile app to see how far away a ride might be, and once you select it, the driver heads in your direction.

If you choose to use a particular ridesharing service, it means that you are only going to be seeing those available ridesharing cars that are perchance signed-up with that service. There might be other ridesharing services that have available cars and those are even closer to your position at the curb, at that moment, but you tend to ignore them and go with the ridesharing service that you prefer.

Suppose in the future that there are zillions of ridesharing cars that are nearby when you happen to go out to the curb. Rather than being focused on one particular ridesharing firm, you might be willing to go with whichever ridesharing car happens to get there soonest. Of course, you also care about the cost, and the quality of the ride, and let's assume for the moment that's a given.

Put on your hat of the firms and individuals that will own AI self-driving cars and are trying to make money by using those self-driving cars as a ridesharing service.

They want to put their AI self-driving car in places that will maximize their revenues of doing ridesharing. This means they want their AI self-driving car to be chosen for a paying fare. They also want to minimize the unused time of their AI self-driving car, which essentially is nonpaying, such as when their AI self-driving car is roaming to find a fare.

If you knew that in say downtown Los Angeles that Wilshire Boulevard will have the greatest number of potential riders between 5 p.m. and 6 p.m. on weekdays, where would you want your AI self-driving car to be?

Well, it's similar to the drivers at the Tuesday events, namely they wanted to be near the action. You would not want your AI self-driving car roaming five blocks away, since another AI self-driving car that's roaming on Wilshire Boulevard is likely going to snag the fare that your AI self-driving car might have been able to get, but your AI self-driving car was not in the right place.

The Future of Ridesharing via AI Self-Driving Cars

Here's what might happen.

All these businesses that have AI self-driving cars are going to want to funnel them into whatever places and at whatever times will earn them the most in fare revenues. Since they all want to do this, you'll have a grand convergence of AI self-driving cars, all flocking to the same places, ones that seem to offer the most chance of getting riders.

For the Tuesday events, recall that the ridesharing cars and taxis figured out on their own via word-of-mouth that it made sense to hangout at the HQ on Tuesday evenings, along with jockeying for physical position. That's exactly what's going to happen with AI self-driving cars that have been put into ridesharing service, which I'd postulate will be most of the AI self-driving cars that will exist on our roadways.

In the downtown Los Angeles quarter, you could have a flood of AI self-driving cars, all jockeying for position. All vying to get those riders. They would swarm like moths to a flame. Those that own those AI self-driving cars don't really care about the traffic snarl, other than if it reduces their chances of their AI self-driving car not making a buck because of the density of competition.

For the human riders that want a ride, it could be a nirvana of choices. Those AI self-driving cars all coming to get you, and presumably the owners might have setup various special discounts and incentives. Use the XYZ ridesharing AI self-driving car that's coming down the street right now, and you'll get a 10% off for picking it, rather than using the ABC ridesharing AI self-driving car that's this moment pulled to the curb where you are standing. Isn't it worth the 10% off to wait another 15 seconds for your ride?

I'd like to also take a momentary step back and ask you to contemplate what this kind of flood of AI self-driving cars will do to the traffic situation.

If you have a belly full of AI self-driving cars trying to all circle around and around among a few blocks area in downtown, the resultant impact to traffic movement will be startling. Gridlock will ensue. Those AI self-driving cars don't care per se about sitting in traffic, which humans tend to avoid. The only thing to curtail the AI self-driving car from sitting in traffic is the opportunity lost of potentially snagging a fare, because the AI self-driving car was stuck in traffic a block from where a rider was seeking to get a ride.

This also brings up another pet peeve of mine.

Pundits keep saying that we won't need parking lots anymore, due to the emergence of AI self-driving cars. The logic seems to be that your AI self-driving car will roam while you aren't using it. It won't park. Instead, it just keeps roaming.

Keep in mind there is a cost involved in having your AI self-driving car roaming. For each minute or hour that it is underway, it is like any car that will be encountering wear and tear. There is also the cost of the electrical power that it is consuming, if an EV, or the cost of gasoline if conventionally powered. This constant roaming is not cost free.

And, as per my earlier comments, your roaming AI self-driving car is going to be plugging up traffic. All of those roaming AI self-driving cars are going to mean more cars on tight city streets. I dare say that most pundits don't seem to realize what this continual roaming will do. I'll also mention that this continual roaming will have a damaging effect on the roadways, which is another cost that needs to be considered (at least for the entities that maintain the roadway infrastructure).

My view is that we are going to need to have waiting areas for AI self-driving cars, essentially parking lots. This would be akin to what you see done at airports. There are ridesharing and taxi waiting areas that are parking lots, though the cars might be moving slowly or waiting in line, and they gradually are released from the waiting area to go to where they can pick-up fares.

Some pundits would say that sure, go ahead and create those waiting areas (parking lots), but put them further away from say the downtown area. You can maybe get cheaper land outside of the downtown, and it can be unused property that nobody otherwise wants to use (abandoned cow pastures made into a waiting area?), since it isn't in downtown, and have the roaming AI self-driving cars sit there.

I ask you, how does that square with the idea that the owners of those AI self-driving cars want their self-driving cars to be in the places that will maximize their fares?

If my AI self-driving car is sitting in a waiting area that's twenty minutes from downtown Los Angeles, it is not going to make much money, especially in comparison to a competitor that has their AI self-driving car driving around and around in the downtown streets to snag fares. Plus, even if it gets a reservation to go pick-up a fare, you now have the cost of the AI self-driving car going the twenty minutes from the waiting area to downtown (and, the cost of when the AI self-driving car went to the waiting area to begin with).

My point being that it seems doubtful to believe that you can relinquish back all of the parking lots in congested areas by either betting on roaming AI self-driving cars or by thinking that you'll simply relegate the AI self-driving cars to sitting outside of town in some non-congested place and waiting to be hailed.

We all need to be thinking more clearly about these matters. Shortcuts as a way of thinking is going to make for larger problems.

Precision Scheduling of Autonomous and Human-Based Ridesharing (PSAHBR)

I had mentioned that the Tuesday evening desperation of taxis and ridesharing services was somewhat dealt with by doing things in a more planned way. Similarly, the freight train hubs are going to be transformed into a more rigorous and systematic form of coordination, via the PSR (Precision Scheduling Railroading).

One solution to the AI self-driving car flood of ridesharing might be to consider putting in place a kind of universal Precision Scheduling of Autonomous and Human-Based Ridesharing (PSAHBR) system.

In essence, ridesharing services would put into inventory of this universal scheduling system their AI self-driving cars as an available ridesharing vehicle. The system would then try to schedule the placement of the AI self-driving cars to meet demand.

It will be a complicated algorithm, that's for sure.

In a manner of speaking, it is reminiscent of the National Resident Matching Program (NRMP), often referred to as The Match, which occurs in the United States and involves the matching of U.S. medical school students into the available residency programs at teaching hospitals each year.

A non-profit non-governmental entity was setup to do this. If you aren't aware of it, you might want to look online about the matter, and it uses a famous problem known as the "stable marriage problem" as an underlying way to find an algorithm to deal with the matching process.

The mighty PSAHBR would be a kind of matching that involves the pairing of those seeking a ride with an available ridesharing car. Notice that I did not say that it would necessarily be an AI self-driving ridesharing car that is only in the inventory of the PSAHBR system.

As I've mentioned earlier, we are going to have a mixture of human driven cars and AI self-driving cars for quite a while. If you were to design the PSAHBR for solely dealing with the assignment of AI self-driving cars, it would mean that the human driven ridesharing cars would not be included.

Those human driven ridesharing cars could then potentially poach the rides that the AI self-driving cars are trying to get. Or, you would have a backlash of the human driven ridesharing cars that those human drivers are being discriminated against by the AI self-driving car availabilities, and perhaps the human drivers weren't able to get rides that were instead being handed to the AI self-driving cars.

Presumably, the PSAHBR would smoothen out the traffic situation and aim to reduce the continual and somewhat wasteful aspects of ridesharing roaming, whether by human drivers or by AI self-driving cars. The system would need to have an indication of where riders tend to want rides, and by using Machine Learning and Deep Learning could try to predict when rides are needed, along with figuring out optimal ways to arrange for the ridesharing inventory to be available at the right places at the right times.

One question right away that one needs to ask involves whether those that own the ridesharing cars are going to voluntarily seek to use such a system. It all depends.

If the PSAHBR can do a good enough job of scheduling, it would imply that the owners of the ridesharing services will earn more revenue and have less cost than if they had tried to just let their ridesharing cars roam. Obviously, the owners would be making a decision about whether it is better to go free or to use the system.

That being the case, there might be localities that decide to force the ridesharing services to use such a system. Akin to my earlier indication about airports, the airport authority is able to ban ridesharing from freely entering into the airport and force the ridesharing services to comply to the rules that are established. Presumably, a city could do likewise.

Who would put in place the PSAHBR? It could be a non-profit non-governmental entity that was established to create and keep in shape such a system. Or, it could be a governmental agency that opts to do so.

One would certainly expect that the major ridesharing services would be tending to craft something like this anyway, if nothing else to try and watch over their own fleets. Would other fleets join in? Would the mom-and-pop cottage industry join in? Likely it would depend upon the perceived "fairness" of how the ridesharing cars are given fares.

Conclusion

Whatever does happen in the future, I think it is a reasonable bet that once AI self-driving cars become prevalent, there will be a swirling of ridesharing that will make our heads spin. At first, it might seem like a welcomed capability. After things turn ugly due to the overabundance of ridesharing, there will be a wringing of the hands about what to do.

The public and the regulators are likely to realize that something needs to be done, once traffic snarls emerge and there is a cutthroat vying for fares. Can someone get all of the ridesharing services to voluntarily come together into a universal scheduling system, or will it require a more heavy hand to do so?

Time will tell. Meanwhile, for those of you that are interested in developing new and innovative apps, consider the kind of scheduling system that the PSAHBR would be, and get coding.

CHAPTER 7
HUMAN DRIVING
EXTINCTION
AND
AI SELF-DRIVING CARS

CHAPTER 7

HUMAN DRIVING
EXTINCTION
AND
AI SELF-DRIVING CARS

What is your relationship with driving?

Kind of a curious question, I realize, but it goes to the heart of the matter about whether you are someone that craves being able to drive a car or instead consider driving to be a burdensome task that happens to be a necessity. Ponder for a moment where you fall on the spectrum of driving interests, consisting at one end of the gamut are those that are extremely passionate about being able to drive and at the other end are those that would just as soon not drive if they could avoid doing so (perhaps even abhorring the act of driving).

When I was in college, I had one friend that loved to drive. He would drive a car for any reason whatsoever.

One day, we wanted to go to the lower part of the campus, which involved about a five-minute walk, an easy downhill jaunt from the upper campus, and he offered to drive instead of walking. This was kind of crazy because we would first have needed to walk to the parking lot that housed his car, and once he drove us down to the lower part of campus, he'd need to park in another parking lot down there.

In the end, we would have ended-up walking to and from the campus parking lots, which was a cumulative total distance greater than if we simply walked directly to the building on the lower campus that we wanted to visit.

It didn't matter to him, since he was focused on driving. He relished driving. No matter how short or far a distance involved.

On another occasion, we were joking about driving from Los Angeles up to Berkeley to visit the famous Cal campus up there, possibly doing so because we had heard that there was a pizza place near the UC Berkeley campus that had the best slices in California. This would be a six-hour drive, in each direction, driving up and driving back down. We were joking about it. He offered to go and get us some of that pizza. The drive time was an attractor to him, allowing him to have even more time behind the wheel.

When I was first learning to drive, I remember that my grandmother was someone that did not favor the act of driving. She sternly cautioned me that I should avoid driving on freeways. Her logic was that the freeway was a last resort way to get to someplace and the speeds were so dangerous that I should take side streets instead of using the freeway. She also counseled me to try and group together my driving tasks, doing them back-to-back, rather than going on separate trips. This advice was based on the notion that I would then be on the roadways as a driver for a lesser amount of time.

For the getting of groceries, my grandmother would drive to the local grocery store once per month, buy all the supplies she needed for about a month, and then drive home. The distance each way was maybe five miles. Not very far at all.

Yet, she hated driving and was only doing the once monthly trip as an absolute "survival" necessity, getting the food and other items that she needed for a month at a time. If you sat in the car as she drove, you could see her hands clutching the steering wheel with a deathlike grip, her head pushed forward, her eyes intently scanning the surroundings, and the sweat coming down her forehead as she clearly disliked having to drive.

In between those that love to drive and those that hate to drive are those that are somewhat ambivalent about driving. They will drive as needed, not fearing it, nor craving it. Essentially, driving is a chore. When the chore needs to be undertaken, so be it. No qualms. If they were to choose between driving a car and not driving a car, it would be an economic kind of decision as to whether driving was a more rational way to get to their destination or not.

I was working at a major entertainment company based in Hollywood and the firm opted to have a New York City (NYC) based executive of the firm switch to working in Los Angeles. When he first arrived, I met with him and we chatted about the differences between Los Angeles and NYC. He mentioned that he did not own a car. I told him that having a car in Los Angeles is pretty much a must-have.

He then somewhat embarrassingly told me that he had never driven a car. Having grown-up in NYC, he had never seen a need to learn to drive. He normally used the NYC subways and cabs and felt that driving a car was unnecessary for him. He hoped that in Los Angeles he could use our public transportation system and ridesharing to get around. I politely indicated that unlike NYC, the Los Angeles area is not really a mass transit kind of place, and the odds were that he'd eventually realize that driving is a fundamental condition of living here.

Within about two months, he got his driver's license, started actively driving, and bought a car. That's Los Angeles for you.

Driving Is A Privilege, Not A Right

For those that do drive a car, they often are quite strong willed about their perceived "right" to drive.

There are some people that seem to think that driving a car is a constitutional right, which is a misnomer. I am not sure why there are people that believe they have a right to drive. I've heard some claim that it is a basic or foundational right of all humans. Some say that driving is a core aspect of freedom, meaning that we are apparently all born to be free and driving is part of that moral immutable all-mankind code.

Let's be clear that by-and-large there is no viable "right" of driving. It is not in the constitution. In the United States, driving is considered a privilege. This means that there is a governmental authority, usually the states, upon which there is a granting of the privilege to their citizens that they can drive a car.

Since it is a privilege, this also means that the granting authority can invoke it, or the authority can revoke it, or the authority can suspend it. Most states have requirements for you to be granted the privilege to drive, including requiring you to take a test, provide evidence of insurance, and take other steps to fulfill the stated requirements. Once you've jumped through the needed hoops, you are granted the driving privilege.

If you abuse the privilege and violate the restrictions, the granting authority can opt to suspend your privilege of driving. For example, this could happen if you are caught and convicted of drunk driving or being DUI.

There are many ways in which you might have your driving privilege suspended. Likewise, the granting authority can revoke your driving privilege altogether. In some rarer instances, your driving license might have driving impositions imposed, rather than being suspended or outright revoked.

Once your driving privilege is suspended or revoked, or if you never had it invoked to begin with, it is generally illegal for you to be driving a car. I point this out because there is nothing that physically bars you from driving a car per se. You could still get behind the wheel, but you'd be driving unlawfully. In California, someone caught driving without a valid driver's license is subject to being prosecuted as a criminal and could get up to one year of jail time.

There is another myth about driving that many people harbor, namely that they falsely believe that the privilege of driving applies only to driving on public roads. These people are apt to quickly claim that they can drive without a driver's license as long as they do so on a private road or on any private property. I hear people say this quite often.

They could be mistaken. It is up to each state in the USA to decide what posture the state wishes to take as a granting authority about the driver license requirements concerning private roads and private properties. In Mississippi, it is against the law to drive DUI anywhere, including both public and private property. In Connecticut, driving recklessly is banned on both public and private property. Overall, the granting authorities tend to have various rules about public versus private property, providing a bit more leniency or exceptions if you are driving on private property.

Sometimes there is confusion too about what private property consists of, in comparison to public property. You drive your car on public roads to a local mall. The mall is owned by a private company. Once you drive from the public roads onto the mall property, and drive around the mall parking lot, are you now driving on private property or public property?

You would be tempted to say that you are driving on private property. That's not often the case. In California, a private property that is open to the public, such as a mall parking lot, becomes bound generally by the rules of driving that apply to public property. The logic being that the private property is being used in a manner consistent with a public property, and therefore the state wants to ensure that the driving there be under the umbrella of public property driving rules.

Being Protective Of The Driving Privilege

My college buddy would have told you that he would fight to the ends of the earth to keep his privilege to drive. My grandmother, in spite of her hesitation about driving, would nearly be as earnest in her support for the privilege to drive. Whether you like driving or not, most people seem to be willing to acknowledge that driving is something that people should be able to do, as long as they do so responsibly.

My children were eager to get their driver's licenses. In our society, earning the privilege of driving is a kind of rites of passage. There were many of their peers that wanted to get a driver's license, even though they had little or no intention of actually driving, at least not right away. Having a driver's license suggests that you have become an adult, though the requirements often don't require that you must have reached the legally stipulated age of an adult. It is a cultural notion of adulthood.

I had used the word freedom earlier. For many drivers, the privilege of driving is a form of personal freedom. It provides a vital personal means of mobility. They can go where they want, when they want, and don't need to rely upon others to do so. When my grandmother got older and was no longer a viable driver, it was devastating to her that she no longer had the privilege to drive. It was more than the act of driving, it was her spirit and view of the world was wrapped into the capability of being able to drive a car.

The act of driving involves not merely the technical motions of maneuvering a car, it also includes a basket of other societal and cultural elements. You might drive because you enjoy it. You might drive because it gets you to work. You might drive because you can. You might drive to show-off to your friends. You might drive to socialize with others. You might drive to rush to a hospital because you need urgent care. And so on.

Currently, we are a car focused society. It permeates most aspects of our daily lives.

There are some analysts that say we are perhaps weaning away from driving and toward being driven.

Gen Z is said to be eschewing owning a car. They are growing up with a ridesharing approach to transportation. This means that they are used to someone else doing the driving. This seems to be fine with many in the Gen Z segment. Baby boomers and Gen X appear to be continuing to cling to their driving privilege.

This raises in interesting question. Will the newest generation and future generations perceive the act of driving in a different way than most of the rest of us do today?

As the existing and older generations expire, will society shift toward a less vital perspective about individuals being able to drive? Maybe society will consider driving a "profession" such as being a chauffeur, like a cab driver or a ridesharing driver, and the everyday person won't drive, or not drive much.

When this topic comes up, there are some that will exclaim that you will take away their driving privilege over their dead body. You will pry the steering wheel from their cold dead hands. That kind of resistance is often heatedly offered.

Why would there be a potential movement to somehow undermine the driving privileges that we enjoy today?

What stokes these passionate drivers about being upset of having their driving "rights" denied to them?

As I'll describe in a moment, the topic of AI self-driving cars often gets this kind of visceral reaction about human driving as a potential for being on the chopping block. Some are worried, very worried, seriously worried, gravely worried that human driving might become extinct.

AI Self-Driving Cars And The Human Driving Debate

What does this have to do with AI self-driving cars?

At the Cybernetic AI Self-Driving Car Institute, we are developing AI software for self-driving cars. At many AI and Autonomous Vehicles (AV) conferences, attendees often bring up whether or not human driving is going to last or not. This is a topic that can rapidly devolve into a muddied shouting match. I'd like to instead offer some calm thoughts on the matter.

Allow me to elaborate.

I'd like to first clarify and introduce the notion that there are varying levels of AI self-driving cars. The topmost level is considered Level 5. A Level 5 self-driving car is one that is being driven by the AI and there is no human driver involved. For the design of Level 5 self-driving cars, the auto makers are even removing the gas pedal, brake pedal, and steering wheel, since those are contraptions used by human drivers. The Level 5 self-driving car is not being driven by a human and nor is there an expectation that a human driver will be present in the self-driving car. It's all on the shoulders of the AI to drive the car.

For self-driving cars less than a Level 5, there must be a human driver present in the car. The human driver is currently considered the responsible party for the acts of the car. The AI and the human driver are co-sharing the driving task.

In spite of this co-sharing, the human is supposed to remain fully immersed into the driving task and be ready at all times to perform the driving task. I've repeatedly warned about the dangers of this co-sharing arrangement and predicted it will produce many untoward results.

Let's focus herein on the true Level 5 self-driving car. Much of the comments apply to the less than Level 5 self-driving cars too, but the fully autonomous AI self-driving car will receive the most attention in this discussion.

Here's the usual steps involved in the AI driving task:

- Sensor data collection and interpretation

- Sensor fusion

- Virtual world model updating

- AI action planning

- Car controls command issuance

Another key aspect of AI self-driving cars is that they will be driving on our roadways in the midst of human driven cars too. There are some pundits of AI self-driving cars that continually refer to a utopian world in which there are only AI self-driving cars on the public roads. Currently there are about 250+ million conventional cars in the United States alone, and those cars are not going to magically disappear or become true Level 5 AI self-driving cars overnight.

Indeed, the use of human driven cars will last for many years, likely many decades, and the advent of AI self-driving cars will occur while there are still human driven cars on the roads. This is a crucial point since this means that the AI of self-driving cars needs to be able to contend with not just other AI self-driving cars, but also contend with human driven cars.

It is easy to envision a simplistic and rather unrealistic world in which all AI self-driving cars are politely interacting with each other and being civil about roadway interactions. That's not what is going to be happening for the foreseeable future. AI self-driving cars and human driven cars will need to be able to cope with each other. Period.

Returning to the topic of driving as a human privilege, let's consider the various ways in which this topic comes up when also discussing AI self-driving cars.

Some Claim To Replace Human Drivers Entirely By AI Self-Driving Cars

I'll begin with the elephant in the room. There seems to be a contingent of pundits that often will get people agitated by saying that we should replace all human drivers with AI self-driving cars.

When stated in that manner, it certainly seems like a rather stark proposition. Definitely has the potential to get the blood boiling.

The rationale is usually predicated on the belief that AI self-driving cars will be safer as drivers than are humans. It is assumed by these pundits that by eliminating human drivers, there will be a complete elimination of all driving related injuries, deaths, and property damages that come from car accidents or incidents.

This is the Holy Grail of AI self-driving cars, at least according to such pundits.

We ought to carefully unpack such an incendiary claim.

The first point to consider involves the timeframe involved in this claim. The proposition is often stated as though starting tomorrow we will round-up all driver's licenses and toss them into a mighty bonfire. For those of you that relish driving your car, apparently by the end of the week you'll no longer ever get to touch a steering wheel or use the pedals of a car, again, ever again. Sorry, but it's for the good of society, tough luck to you.

I think this is either unintentionally (or sometimes intentionally) used to get a knee-jerk reaction and have a shock effect. That being said, I know some that have lost a loved one via a car accident, and for which they are desirous that no one else ever suffer such a loss, therefore the AI self-driving car seems like a welcome way to ensure that others don't have to undergo what they have had to deal with. Those people are doing what is in their hearts, and sincerely believe in the idea of getting human drivers out-of-the-loop of driving.

The thing is, realistically we are decades (at least) away from being able to even consider doing what they are proposing.

There are about 250 million cars in the United States today. About 15 million or so new cars are sold each year in the United States. If we had true Level 5 AI self-driving cars, how many years would it take to gradually do away with the existing stock of conventional cars and bring into the marketplace the new Level 5 self-driving cars?

Would we need to replace all 250 million conventional cars with the same number of AI self-driving cars? Some argue that with the gradually shifting trend towards a desire to use ridesharing, we presumably won't need to replace all 250 million conventional cars and some lesser number of AI self-driving cars would suffice, since they would be used on a shared basis.

Okay, if that's the case, how many AI self-driving cars would there need to be in circulation? It still has to be into the many millions of cars, double-digit or low three-digits, so let's pretend for argument sake that it is say 100 million such AI self-driving cars.

Do you realize how long it would take to make that many cars? And how long it would take for people or companies to purchase such cars and put them into use?

There is a thing known as AI self-driving cars at scale.

This means going far beyond merely handfuls or hundreds of AI self-driving cars and moving toward having thousands and hundreds of thousands of them. Millions is a whole another level of scaling. We are right now working on the baby steps. Dealing with millions upon millions of AI self-driving cars is very far off on the horizon.

It is an act of fiction to simply assume that if you can make one AI self-driving car that you can just crank out millions of them and put them onto our roads. This is a fallacy of logic.

There is another perspective that says the number of AI self-driving cars might become even higher than the number of conventional cars in-place today. In essence, maybe we might end-up with maybe 300 million AI self-driving cars and no convention cars, over time. Why?

Because there is the "law" of induced demand. When you make available a new means of transportation, what can happen is that the suppressed need of transportation can emerge. This implies that there is a possibility that the existing base of conventional cars is insufficient to meet the total demand that will emerge once AI self-driving cars arise.

The counter-argument is that the conventional car of today is not especially being shared. The shared aspects of an AI self-driving car, assuming it will be shared, would suggest that the AI self-driving car can meet more driving demand than does a conventional car. Also, the AI self-driving car can be used 7x24, whereas conventional cars are "limited" to needing a human driver, which is not as readily viable.

I defy you to provide an economic means by which any this would happen in any short time frame on the scale of allowing society to stop all human driving and rely instead on AI self-driving cars.

It really doesn't square out.

This means that when you start saying that there won't be any more human driving, due to the advent of AI self-driving cars, you are really talking about something that might happen many decades from now, maybe.

Furthermore, we don't really know what society might be like by the time that such a possibility even might be available. Flying cars? Personal jet packs? Mass transit unlike the kind that we know of today? There are so many changes bound to happen that it is not contextually sensible to claim that we would overnight stop people from driving.

It could be that by the time the advent of mass-scale use of AI self-driving cars arises, people won't be doing conventional driving very much anyway. There might be an ongoing shift in society toward not driving a car. Thus, by the time that there is an initiative to close off human driving, few will care much about it anyway.

My point is that having an argument about needing to give-up your privilege of driving, due to the pervasive adoption of AI self-driving cars, sufficiently to overcome the loss of human driving and yet still meet driving demand, it is premature to argue as though this is real, and instead it is merely an abstract proposition, which might or might not come to fruition at some far-off future.

Narrower Elimination of Human Driving

I've tried to make the case that a full-scale whole-hog elimination of human driving as a result of the emergence of AI self-driving cars is not in the cards as yet, and it is a distant future idea, which we can only speculate about.

161

Some worry about it now, some don't. Some say let's cross that bridge when there are actually viable signs that the bridge is actually up ahead. Others say that it is worthwhile to ponder what might be in the future, regardless of how far ahead it might be and no matter how theoretical the debate might be.

There are some pundits that once they are presented with such a view and the suggestion that the urgency or near-term does not seem to encompass the outlawing entirely of human driving, not in any practical sense, will recast how the elimination of human driving might happen.

In this recast perspective, the scope of elimination might be narrowed, so let's consider that alternative.

Suppose the emergence of AI self-driving cars suggests such autonomous vehicles can work safely and appropriately on our roadways, but maybe only best when geofenced and kept to areas that are comprehensively mapped and understood. Rather than using them everywhere, perhaps they are limited to being used in certain areas. A downtown area might declare that henceforth there are only AI self-driving cars allowed to drive in their downtown area. No human driven cars allowed.

Does this mean that human drivers are going to lose their privilege to drive?

Not really. It means that you cannot drive a car while inside the downtown area. You can still drive a car on the freeways, highways, and streets that are outside of the downtown area.

I realize you might get upset about the restriction of not being able to drive while in the downtown area, but this seems to be not be much of a valid complaint. There are many areas that already restrict the driving of cars and instead have local shuttles, buses, rental bikes, scooters, and encourage walking rather than driving.

You won't get much sympathy from me about your being prevented from driving your car in that downtown area. Live with it. You still have the driving privilege. You can still drive while outside of the downtown area.

Some though tell me that they are worried this is a kind of slippery slope. First confining step, they cannot drive in a downtown area. Next confining step, it will be that you cannot drive in a suburb area. Next down the rabbit hole, you cannot drive on certain freeways or highways. In a "death by a thousand cuts" manner, your privilege of driving is being eroded.

Some suggest it is all a conspiracy to ultimately rob you of the privilege of driving. As an aside, I'm not much of a fan of conspiracy theories. I doubt that this would be a grand scheme. I do concede though that something like this might happen in an incremental fashion, one slow step at a time, but not due to a sinister secretive underbelly of miscreants having devilish plans.

The time frame is once again decades away, at best. Could though it be the case that a long time from now the only place you can drive a car would be in a few leftover places? Sure, I suppose that is possible.

Some even envision a future whereby the only human driving that will occur involves driving on a closed track. There might be locales that setup closed tracks and let you drive a car, perhaps an old farm converted to a closed track or other expansive property transformed, doing so for the thrill of driving (and as a potential money maker). These would be amusement parks for driving. There are similar kinds of tracks today for those that want to do race car style driving. These future tracks would presumably be used by anyone wanting to simply be able to drive a car, even at a scant five or ten miles per hour, reinvigorating the excitement and joys of driving a car.

There is perhaps an irony about this notion, since today we have AI self-driving cars that make use of closed tracks for providing grounds. Could it really be that someday the AI self-driving cars would drive where we as humans drive today, and the humans of the future would be relegated to only being able to drive on closed tracks that AI self-driving cars once were saddled to use? It's a bit of conjecture, one would say.

In any case, notice that human driving is still being allowed. It is not the complete elimination of human driving.

For those of you determined to keep the driving privilege, you might have a pained expression and be saying that a driving privilege that only applies to driving on specially provided closed tracks or on only the off-the-beaten path roads is not any more a bona fide driving privilege. The restrictions are so severe that it might as well be the wholescale elimination of driving for humans. Well, I get your point, but once again we are debating an obscure possibility that is far away in the future.

Restricting Human Driving for the Sake of AI Self-Driving

One reason that some favor "eliminating" human driving is due to the notion that the AI self-driving car will presumably be able to drive more safely than human drivers. This suggests that AI self-driving cars won't become drunk drivers, since the AI won't be sitting on a barstool and then decide to take the car for a ride. Nor would the AI be presumably distracted by trying to text on a smartphone or be eating a sandwich while trying to drive a car.

Another reason for "eliminating" human driving is due to the potent dangers of mixing human driving with AI self-driving car driving.

You are a passenger in an AI self-driving car. You feel comforted by the aspect that the AI won't get drunk, and it won't get distracted, presumably. I think we all know that the problem about driving is that you can be an extremely safe driver, and yet another car can plow into you. It doesn't really matter how safe you might be, providing lots of driving distance between you and other cars, in the sense that a drunk driver can still come upon your car and ram into you.

I'm not saying that being a safety conscious driver is not a good way to drive, it is a good way to drive. You are reducing the chances of the everyday kinds of car accidents that can happen. I'm merely pointing out that no matter how safe you are, there is the chance that an unsafe driver can still get you.

This implies that even with AI self-driving cars on our roadways, and assuming that they work safely, when you put them in the midst of human driven cars, there is now a chance that a human driven car will somehow contribute to an AI self-driving car getting into an untoward incident. It could be outright, such as a human driven car crashing into an AI self-driving car, or it might be a situation that a human driven car suddenly cuts off an AI self-driving car and the AI self-driving car goes barreling off the road.

As such, there are some that suggest we keep human driven cars away from AI self-driving cars. Or, if you prefer to see it the other way, we keep AI self-driving cars away from human driven cars.

My earlier example of a downtown area that bans human driving is illustrative of this aspect. Similarly, some suggest that we might declare that there are lanes on the freeway that are only for AI self-driving cars and not for human driven cars, akin to how we allocate HOV lanes today. You could do the same for highways, particular streets, and any place that cars might go.

There are some potential hurdles and difficulties with this separation approach.

How do you enforce the separation?

If the separation does not involve physical barriers of separation, it means that human driven cars can still mix with the AI self-driving cars. The human driver might do so illegally, and be subject to a ticket, but nonetheless they are still able to drive where the AI self-driving cars are. This means that you've reduced the chances of mixture incidents, but not eliminated it.

Another approach involves setting up barriers to prevent the human driven cars from getting into the stream of AI self-driving cars. This tends to require substantial changes to the roadway infrastructure. Those kinds of changes will cost money to put in place. How much will we be willing to pay to enforce the physical separation? Will the barriers be sufficient to fully keep out the human driven cars?

There's another reason sometimes given to argue for a separation between the human driven cars and the AI self-driving cars, namely making life easier for the AI self-driving cars.

One of the hardest challenges for AI self-driving cars involves dealing with human driven cars.

In theory, if you had only AI self-driving cars, they would be able to coordinate with each other. They would use V2V (vehicle to vehicle) electronic communication and be able to collaborate while driving in traffic. They would not be likely to ram into each other.

By allowing human driven cars to mix with AI self-driving cars, the AI needs to be a lot cleverer than it would otherwise with only AI self-driving cars in the mix. Some believe that we are being delayed of getting to AI self-driving cars because of the arduous chore of getting them to deal with human driven cars.

Rather than waiting until we can figure out how to deal with human driven cars, some AI developers say that we should just get rid of the human driven cars. This seems like an easy solution. The problem is those pesky human drivers, so get rid of them.

How do you get rid of human drivers? You can separate them away from wherever AI self-driving cars are driving, or you can ban human drivers from driving.

This takes me back to the earlier point about the contentious point often lobbed out that we should no longer allow human driving. Those computer scientists and AI developers that already believe humans are fickle and imperfect, well, it just plain makes sense to take those flaky humans out of the equation. This would allow for AI self-driving cars to be much less burdened and make it a lot easier to program those AI systems.

Think about how nice it would be.

No human drivers implies no drunk human drivers and no distracted human drivers. It means that human drivers won't get in the way of AI self-driving cars that are coordinating among themselves to smoothen traffic flow. You are taking what is otherwise an immense problem and chopping out a huge component that makes the problem really hard.

I try to bring some semblance of reality into such discussions by pointing out that the AI self-driving cars would still need to deal with pedestrians. Believe it or not, there are some AI developers that complain about pedestrians and suggest we should keep pedestrians away from AI self-driving cars. That seems like a tall order, and it is unclear how you would achieve this. In any case, I also bring up the topic of bicyclists, scooter riders, motorcyclists, etc.

Once again, the typical dreamworld answer is that those all be eliminated too. Not sure how that would be plausible.

The only chance you have of doing something like this would be to have roads that are exclusively for use by AI self-driving cars. Some have suggested that we might build freeways that are only for AI self-driving cars. Maybe we could build tunnels and have AI self-driving cars be isolated away from these other "distractions" that make driving difficult.

Those are all potential options. It does increase the overall cost of AI self-driving cars, due to having to build and maintain various specially set aside roads or tunnels for the use of the AI self-driving cars. As a society, we would want to include that infrastructure cost into the adoption cost of AI self-driving cars.

I also often point out that these efforts to make life easier for the AI can become a kind of crutch.

If the AI does not need to be good enough to handle these real-world driving matters, I say that we need to make better AI. Turning things on their head by saying that we should make the environment simpler and easier for the AI is something I'd suggest will impede the effort toward making the AI fully capable at the driving task.

You might want to argue that we could temporarily use as a stopgap measure the less-clever AI self-driving cars on roads by restricting the driving environment. What would be the cost for that short-term Band-Aid solution? How long would we then go until we improved the AI to undo the needed restricted driving environments?

I'd need to see some kind of cost-benefit analysis that would showcase the value of proceeding with the restricted environment approach over waiting until we had the fuller AI self-driving cars available. Per my earlier suggestion about a crutch, would the time period of using the restricted environment tend to reduce the pressure towards making better AI, and if so would we be making a tradeoff that is worthwhile in doing so?

Some Extra Parts Of The Debate

I'll include a few more aspects about this debate that are perhaps extraneous, or one might say are less than the mainstream of such discussions.

One aspect is that we might all become so comfortable with AI self-driving cars and be relieved to not be driving and be overjoyed at being able to use the time while inside an AI self-driving car for other more useful purposes, we won't want to do driving.

Human driving will be eliminated by choice, by the advent of something so much better that no one will want to do human driving.

It is like debating about keeping your shovel to be able to dig a hole, yet if everyone was given an automated digging machine, why would any reasonable person cling to their primitive shovel? Once you've gotten a proven alternative that is readily available, the picture of what you might choose is changed. During the time that there are only shovels, and not yet the automated digging machines, people would rightfully argue that you cannot take away their shovel. Doing so would leave them without a viable means to dig.

Some would say that not everyone will necessarily be of the same mind about this overjoy for AI self-driving cars and there will still be some "extremists" that will want to drive, in spite of the preponderance of society willingly and eagerly embracing AI self-driving cars. For that tiny percentage of malcontents, the thinking is they would be able to do the kind of closed track driving that I've earlier offered as a means to still be considered a human driver.

Another perspective is that humans will in a manner of speaking still be doing driving, even if there are AI self-driving cars, and simply be driving via their voices, rather than their hands, arms, and feet.

When you are inside an AI self-driving car, there will be Natural Language Processing (NLP) capabilities like an Alexa or Siri, allowing you to verbally indicate where you want to go. You can also presumably tell the AI self-driving car to stop at the curb up ahead. Aren't you then driving the car? You might not be at the actual steering wheel or pedals, but you are nonetheless doing driving.

The counter-argument is that you are not truly driving the car when you are merely offering commands. Today, if you get into a cab or a ridesharing car and you tell the human driver where to go or when to come to a stop, you aren't driving. You are only offering suggestions to a driver. Therefore, claiming that you are a human driver when in an AI self-driving car that is being driven by the AI is disingenuous, some would assert.

Another angle is that you might be able to do pretend driving via the use of Augmented Reality (AR) or Virtual Reality (VR).

You get into an AI self-driving car and put on special AR glasses or a VR headset, or perhaps the front windshield is your portal for the AR or VR, and the AI starts to drive the self-driving car. You are able to be seated inside the AI self-driving car at a set of virtual or make-believe driving controls. The AI is doing the driving, you are not. But you have the sensation that you are driving, it makes you believe you are driving, and you feel exhilarated to be able to do so.

As you can imagine, not many of those that are in the human driving camp are very enamored of this AR or VR approach. They say it is like putting a baby in a car seat, inside a car, and the baby is given a plastic toy wheel, elated to be "driving" the car, when of course the baby is not doing anything of the kind. This concept of the AR or VR for adult humans as a means to pretend they are driving is said to be both insulting and outright demeaning.

Conclusion

Mark Twain indicated that the reports of his death were greatly exaggerated, doing so when an obituary about him was published in a major newspaper.

I would suggest that the elimination of human driving is akin to that same kind of exaggeration.

Besides my points about any such extinction being quite far off in the future, if it should arise, and also that society might no longer care as much about human driving, you can likely add to the matter that there would be protests aiming to prevent or delay the loss of the driving privilege, there might be lawsuits to prevent the elimination of human driving, and it could become a political hot potato that might get political leaders and regulators earnestly involved and trying to ascertain what the "will of the people" might be about the matter.

We also need to consider whether humans would still be driving but perhaps do so on private property, rather than public property. I know that for those that are ardent human driving proponents, being relegated to driving only on private property is an insult and being treated like a second-class citizen. Got it.

There are some that also worry about the deskilling of humans as it relates to driving. If driving gets restricted or eliminated, would humans "lose" the skill of driving. And if so, would this make us humans vulnerable to technology, meaning that only AI could do our driving. We could become slaves to technology since we cannot drive, even if we wanted to drive, because we no longer know how to drive.

I'd say that you are starting to head into the wilds of science fiction stories. In any case, it seems that we as humans are relatively easily able to drive a car. The barrier to entry of driving a car is quite low. Suggesting that we would become deskilled and not be able to take-up driving again, well, it isn't brain surgery (even though it is a hard thing to get AI to do!).

Should you stay awake at night so that you can worry about the extinction of human driving?

I'd say no. Of the many potential nightmares to keep you awake, I don't think that the elimination of human drivers should be on your list.

You can have comfort that during your lifetime, the odds are quite high that no one is going to take away your driving privilege. There might be some restrictions, such as not letting you drive where AI self-driving cars are driving, but this is likely going to be decades from now.

There is even a chance that you might gradually become less enthused about driving. You might find yourself driving less and less of the time, making use instead of AI self-driving cars. For your peace of mind, you'd still have that driver's license in your pocket, and it probably will still be a rite of passage for teenagers. There are some traditions that will be harder to ease out of.

.

APPENDIX

APPENDIX A
TEACHING WITH THIS MATERIAL

The material in this book can be readily used either as a supplemental to other content for a class, or it can also be used as a core set of textbook material for a specialized class. Classes where this material is most likely used include any classes at the college or university level that want to augment the class by offering thought provoking and educational essays about AI and self-driving cars.

In particular, here are some aspects for class use:

o   Computer Science. Studying AI, autonomous vehicles, etc.

o   Business. Exploring technology and it adoption for business.

o   Sociology. Sociological views on the adoption and advancement of technology.

Specialized classes at the undergraduate and graduate level can also make use of this material.

For each chapter, consider whether you think the chapter provides material relevant to your course topic. There is plenty of opportunity to get the students thinking about the topic and force them to decide whether they agree or disagree with the points offered and positions taken. I would also encourage you to have the students do additional research beyond the chapter material presented (I provide next some suggested assignments they can do).

RESEARCH ASSIGNMENTS ON THESE TOPICS

Your students can find background material on these topics, doing so in various business and technical publications. I list below the top ranked AI related journals. For business publications, I would suggest the usual culprits such as the Harvard Business Review, Forbes, Fortune, WSJ, and the like.

Here are some suggestions of homework or projects that you could assign to students:

a) Assignment for foundational AI research topic: Research and prepare a paper and a presentation on a specific aspect of Deep AI, Machine Learning, ANN, etc. The paper should cite at least 3 reputable sources. Compare and contrast to what has been stated in this book.

b) Assignment for the Self-Driving Car topic: Research and prepare a paper and Self-Driving Cars. Cite at least 3 reputable sources and analyze the characterizations. Compare and contrast to what has been stated in this book.

c) Assignment for a Business topic: Research and prepare a paper and a presentation on businesses and advanced technology. What is hot, and what is not? Cite at least 3 reputable sources. Compare and contrast to the depictions in this book.

d) Assignment to do a Startup: Have the students prepare a paper about how they might startup a business in this realm. They must submit a sound Business Plan for the startup. They could also be asked to present their Business Plan and so should also have a presentation deck to coincide with it.

You can certainly adjust the aforementioned assignments to fit to your particular needs and the class structure. You'll notice that I ask for 3 reputable cited sources for the paper writing based assignments. I usually steer students toward "reputable" publications, since otherwise they will cite some oddball source that has no credentials other than that they happened to write something and post it onto the Internet. You can define "reputable" in whatever way you prefer, for example some faculty think Wikipedia is not reputable while others believe it is reputable and allow students to cite it.

The reason that I usually ask for at least 3 citations is that if the student only does one or two citations they usually settle on whatever they happened to find the fastest. By requiring three citations, it usually seems to force them to look around, explore, and end-up probably finding five or more, and then whittling it down to 3 that they will actually use.

I have not specified the length of their papers, and leave that to you to tell the students what you prefer. For each of those assignments, you could end-up with a short one to two pager, or you could do a dissertation length paper. Base the length on whatever best fits for your class, and the credit amount of the assignment within the context of the other grading metrics you'll be using for the class.

I mention in the assignments that they are to do a paper and prepare a presentation. I usually try to get students to present their work. This is a good practice for what they will do in the business world. Most of the time, they will be required to prepare an analysis and present it. If you don't have the class time or inclination to have the students present, then you can of course cut out the aspect of them putting together a presentation.

If you want to point students toward highly ranked journals in AI, here's a list of the top journals as reported by *various citation counts sources* (this list changes year to year):

o   Communications of the ACM

o   Artificial Intelligence

o   Cognitive Science

o   IEEE Transactions on Pattern Analysis and Machine Intelligence

o   Foundations and Trends in Machine Learning

o   Journal of Memory and Language

o   Cognitive Psychology

o   Neural Networks

o   IEEE Transactions on Neural Networks and Learning Systems

o   IEEE Intelligent Systems

o   Knowledge-based Systems

GUIDE TO USING THE CHAPTERS

For each of the chapters, I provide next some various ways to use the chapter material. You can assign the tasks as individual homework assignments, or the tasks can be used with team projects for the class. You can easily layout a series of assignments, such as indicating that the students are to do item "a" below for say Chapter 1, then "b" for the next chapter of the book, and so on.

a) What is the main point of the chapter and describe in your own words the significance of the topic,

b) Identify at least two aspects in the chapter that you agree with, and support your concurrence by providing at least one other outside researched item as support; make sure to explain your basis for disagreeing with the aspects,

c) Identify at least two aspects in the chapter that you disagree with, and support your disagreement by providing at least one other outside researched item as support; make sure to explain your basis for disagreeing with the aspects,

d) Find an aspect that was not covered in the chapter, doing so by conducting outside research, and then explain how that aspect ties into the chapter and what significance it brings to the topic,

e) Interview a specialist in industry about the topic of the chapter, collect from them their thoughts and opinions, and readdress the chapter by citing your source and how they compared and contrasted to the material,

f) Interview a relevant academic professor or researcher in a college or university about the topic of the chapter, collect from them their thoughts and opinions, and readdress the chapter by citing your source and how they compared and contrasted to the material,

g) Try to update a chapter by finding out the latest on the topic, and ascertain whether the issue or topic has now been solved or whether it is still being addressed, explain what you come up with.

The above are all ways in which you can get the students of your class involved in considering the material of a given chapter. You could mix things up by having one of those above assignments per each week, covering the chapters over the course of the semester or quarter.

As a reminder, here are the chapters of the book and you can select whichever chapters you find most valued for your particular class:

Chapter Title

Companion Book By This Author

Advances in AI and Autonomous Vehicles: Cybernetic Self-Driving Cars

Practical Advances in Artificial Intelligence (AI) and Machine Learning

by

Dr. Lance B. Eliot, MBA, PhD

This title is available via Amazon and other book sellers

Companion Book By This Author

Self-Driving Cars:
"The Mother of All AI Projects"

by Dr. Lance B. Eliot, MBA, PhD

This title is available via Amazon and other book sellers

Companion Book By This Author

Innovation and Thought Leadership on Self-Driving Driverless Cars

by Dr. Lance B. Eliot, MBA, PhD

This title is available via Amazon and other book sellers

This title is available via Amazon and other book sellers

Lance B. Eliot

Companion Book By This Author

Introduction to
Driverless Self-Driving Cars

by Dr. Lance B. Eliot, MBA, PhD

This title is available via Amazon and other book sellers

Companion Book By This Author

Autonomous Vehicle Driverless
Self-Driving Cars and Artificial Intelligence

by Dr. Lance B. Eliot, MBA, PhD

This title is available via Amazon and other book sellers

<u>Companion Book By This Author</u>
Transformative Artificial Intelligence Driverless Self-Driving Cars
by Dr. Lance B. Eliot, MBA, PhD

<u>Chapter Title</u>

This title is available via Amazon and other book sellers

Companion Book By This Author

Disruptive Artificial Intelligence and Driverless Self-Driving Cars

by Dr. Lance B. Eliot, MBA, PhD

This title is available via Amazon and other book sellers

Companion Book By This Author

State-of-the-Art
AI Driverless Self-Driving Cars
by Dr. Lance B. Eliot, MBA, PhD

This title is available via Amazon and other book sellers

Companion Book By This Author

Top Trends in
AI Self-Driving Cars

by Dr. Lance B. Eliot, MBA, PhD

This title is available via Amazon and other book sellers

<u>Companion Book By This Author</u>

AI Innovations and Self-Driving Cars

by Dr. Lance B. Eliot, MBA, PhD

<u>Chapter Title</u>

This title is available via Amazon and other book sellers

<u>Companion Book By This Author</u>

Crucial Advances for
AI Self-Driving Cars

by Dr. Lance B. Eliot, MBA, PhD

<u>Chapter Title</u>

This title is available via Amazon and other book sellers

This title is available via Amazon and other book sellers

Companion Book By This Author

Pioneering Advances for AI Driverless Cars

by Dr. Lance B. Eliot, MBA, PhD

This title is available via Amazon and other book sellers

Companion Book By This Author

Leading Edge Trends for AI Driverless Cars

by Dr. Lance B. Eliot, MBA, PhD

This title is available via Amazon and other book sellers

This title is available via Amazon and other book sellers

<u>Companion Book By This Author</u>

The Next Wave of
AI Self-Driving Cars

by Dr. Lance B. Eliot, MBA, PhD

<u>Chapter Title</u>

This title is available via Amazon and other book sellers

Companion Book By This Author

Revolutionary Innovations of
AI Self-Driving Cars

by Dr. Lance B. Eliot, MBA, PhD

Chapter Title

This title is available via Amazon and other book sellers

Companion Book By This Author

AI Self-Driving Cars
Breakthroughs

by Dr. Lance B. Eliot, MBA, PhD

<u>Chapter Title</u>

This title is available via Amazon and other book sellers

This title is available via Amazon and other book sellers

<u>Companion Book By This Author</u>

***Ingenious Strides for*
AI Driverless Cars**

by Dr. Lance B. Eliot, MBA, PhD

<u>Chapter Title</u>

This title is available via Amazon and other book sellers

Companion Book By This Author

AI Self-Driving Cars
Inventiveness

by Dr. Lance B. Eliot, MBA, PhD

This title is available via Amazon and other book sellers

Companion Book By This Author

Visionary Secrets of
AI Driverless Cars

by Dr. Lance B. Eliot, MBA, PhD

Chapter Title

This title is available via Amazon and other book sellers

Companion Book By This Author

Spearheading
AI Self-Driving Cars

by Dr. Lance B. Eliot, MBA, PhD

This title is available via Amazon and other book sellers

Lance B. Eliot

Companion Book By This Author

Spurring
AI Self-Driving Cars
by Dr. Lance B. Eliot, MBA, PhD

This title is available via Amazon and other book sellers

Avant-Garde
AI Driverless Cars

by Dr. Lance B. Eliot, MBA, PhD

Chapter Title

1 Eliot Framework for AI Self-Driving Cars

2 Linear Non-Threshold and AI Self-Driving Cars

3 Prediction Equation and AI Self-Driving Cars

4 Modular Autonomous Systems and AI Self-Driving Cars

5 Driver's Licensing and AI Self-Driving Cars

6 Offshoots and Spinoffs and AI Self-Driving Car

7 Depersonalization and AI Self-Driving Cars

This title is available via Amazon and other book sellers

Companion Book By This Author

AI Self-Driving Cars
Evolvement

by Dr. Lance B. Eliot, MBA, PhD

This title is available via Amazon and other book sellers

Companion Book By This Author

AI Driverless Cars
Chrysalis
by Dr. Lance B. Eliot, MBA, PhD

Chapter Title

This title is available via Amazon and other book sellers

ABOUT THE AUTHOR

Dr. Lance B. Eliot, MBA, PhD is the CEO of Techbruim, Inc. and Executive Director of the Cybernetic AI Self-Driving Car Institute, and has over twenty years of industry experience including serving as a corporate officer in a billion dollar firm and was a partner in a major executive services firm. He is also a serial entrepreneur having founded, ran, and sold several high-tech related businesses. He previously hosted the popular radio show *Technotrends* that was also available on American Airlines flights via their in-flight audio program. Author or co-author of a dozen books and over 400 articles, he has made appearances on CNN, and has been a frequent speaker at industry conferences.

A former professor at the University of Southern California (USC), he founded and led an innovative research lab on Artificial Intelligence in Business. Known as the "AI Insider" his writings on AI advances and trends has been widely read and cited. He also previously served on the faculty of the University of California Los Angeles (UCLA), and was a visiting professor at other major universities. He was elected to the International Board of the Society for Information Management (SIM), a prestigious association of over 3,000 high-tech executives worldwide.

He has performed extensive community service, including serving as Senior Science Adviser to the Vice Chair of the Congressional Committee on Science & Technology. He has served on the Board of the OC Science & Engineering Fair (OCSEF), where he is also has been a Grand Sweepstakes judge, and likewise served as a judge for the Intel International SEF (ISEF). He served as the Vice Chair of the Association for Computing Machinery (ACM) Chapter, a prestigious association of computer scientists. Dr. Eliot has been a shark tank judge for the USC Mark Stevens Center for Innovation on start-up pitch competitions, and served as a mentor for several incubators and accelerators in Silicon Valley and Silicon Beach. He served on several Boards and Committees at USC, including having served on the Marshall Alumni Association (MAA) Board in Southern California.

Dr. Eliot holds a PhD from USC, MBA, and Bachelor's in Computer Science, and earned the CDP, CCP, CSP, CDE, and CISA certifications. Born and raised in Southern California, and having traveled and lived internationally, he enjoys scuba diving, surfing, and sailing.

ADDENDUM

AI Driverless Cars
Chrysalis

Practical Advances in Artificial Intelligence (AI)
and Machine Learning

By
Dr. Lance B. Eliot, MBA, PhD

———

For supplemental materials of this book, visit:

www.ai-selfdriving-cars.guru

For special orders of this book, contact:

LBE Press Publishing

Email: LBE.Press.Publishing@gmail.com

www.ingramcontent.com/pod-product-compliance
Lightning Source LLC
Chambersburg PA
CBHW051048050326
40690CB00006B/646